The Golden Age
of
Shotgunning

The Golden Age of Shotgunning

by

BOB HINMAN

WINCHESTER PRESS

Library of Congress Catalog Card Number: 72: 159432

ISBN: 0-87691-043-6

Published by Winchester Press
460 Park Avenue, New York 10022

PRINTED IN THE UNITED STATES OF AMERICA

MY SPECIAL THANKS to Dan Wallace, for consultation and use of his private collection; Major George Nonte, for the original idea and impetus to begin; *Shooting Times* magazine, for allowing excerpts from my "Claybirds" column; and most especially, to Marilyn Owen, friend and secretary, through whose typing, urging, and co-effort the book was finally completed.

For JULIE

May it not be her only inheritance

FOREWORD

BOB HINMAN writes nearly as well as he shoots, and that's saying a lot. But this is not a "how to shoot" book, nor was it written as a primer for the fellow who has hardly used a scattergun. Bob's real aim —and I should know, for we discussed it often during the gestation period—was to combine in a single volume the wealth of new and previously unpublished material he had gathered in nearly twoscore years of research and study.

And much of it *is* new. The already well-researched and documented histories of famous companies are merely mentioned in passing. He explores instead the little-known firms who, although contributing much, have been missed by former historians.

Granted, books without end have been written on the shotgun, but none have ever delved deeply into the "Golden Age" or the many factors affecting and contributing to it. The pages which unfold from here forward contain enough material for an advanced degree on the American shotgun during its most glorious and productive years.

Bob has spent his lifetime with scatterguns, and had the good fortune to spend a lot of years in areas where many of the incidents he describes occurred. Much of the story herein came from the old-timers and their gunning progeny who are still around.

There were probably more brands of shotguns used in America during the Golden Age than any other place and time. Bob's biggest challenge in preparing this book was the compilation of close to four hundred makes of guns, along with data on a good many of them. This list of nearly forgotten names, so familiar almost a century ago, is a great contribution to scattergunning knowledge.

The story scorns twentieth-century developments, but is a storehouse of yesterday's game and games, people and guns—and all that goes with them. As such, it stands as a monument to shotgunners past and present.

MAJ. GEORGE C. NONTE JR.

Preface

THIS book deals with the development of the shotgun and wing shooting in the United States during the last thirty years of the nineteenth century. These three decades constituted a unique period for American sportsmen in general, and shotgunners in particular — a time when the supply of feathered game seemed inexhaustible, seasons were long, limits large or nonexistent, and life simple enough to give people the chance to enjoy them.

It was also a time of rapid technological change. It witnessed the transition from muzzleloader to breechloader, from black powder to smokeless, from hammer gun to hammerless. It saw the introduction or rapid evolution of choke and the fixed shotshell, and while experiencing the first pressure from conservationists, saw the development of trapshooting as we know it today in the transition from live pigeons to glass balls and then clay targets. It marked the end of the shotgun as the hand work of one man, and the beginning of industrial mass manufacture, donimated by Americans.

Because of these circumstances, the wing-shooting skills displayed by the great artists of the day attained a level that had never been matched before and have seldom been surpassed since. Indeed, while the conditions under which the modern scattergunner performs have been strikingly altered, very little significant improvement in either the mechanics or equipment of his sport have occurred since then.

Truly, it was a remarkable period, and precisely because of the social, economic, technological and ecological changes it encompassed, we will never see its like again. I know no better way to characterize it than as "The Golden Age of Shotgunning."

The story is not a simple one to tell. The changes referred to above were often simultaneous and interrelated, and it is as difficult to arrange them chronologically with any precision as it is to pick up any one thread of the story without becoming entangled in others. But because of my lifelong fascination with shotguns and sports that involve them, it has been an absorbing story for me to research and to write. I have tried to set it down as straightforwardly as possible for the benefit of other shotgunners who would like to know how it really was during the Golden Age, and hope they get as much pleasure from reading these pages as I did from writing them.

Peoria, Illinois
September, 1971

BOB HINMAN

Contents

The Golden Age
of
Shotgunning

CHAPTER ONE

The Hunting Scene

THE story of the Golden Age of Shotgunning is a complex one, a tale which can be told in many different ways and approached from many different directions. But only as a personal choice, I'd like to begin by looking at the Golden Age from the hunter's viewpoint, and to start off near home in that area around the Illinois River about forty miles south of Peoria where I still go duck hunting. For this was one of the birthplaces of what has been termed a "strictly American institution" — the duck club, the institution that has lent to names like Stuttgart, Aransas Pass, Currituck Sound and Chesapeake a romance that still conjures up visions in the dreams of duck hunters.

The duck clubs still exist today. Their clubhouses range from tarpaper shacks to column-faced mansions, the latter once the domain of millionaires and now, by right of inheritance, the week-end haunts of their graying sons and grandsons, trying to recapture some of the thrill and grandeur of opening days past.

The bags are likely to be small these days, for it does not take long to "limit out" even if the spring hatch in Canada was favorable.

Limits are small and strictly adhered to, for there is constant surveillance from federal and state wardens. Gone are most of the club servants; only a "pusher" or two is needed to set out and pick up the small number of decoys needed to fill the day's bag.

Yes, there are still ducks here in fall and spring, but the once great duck clubs are fighting for survival. The polluted Illinois River itself no longer grows food necessary to support the diving ducks — the bluebills and canvasbacks. Only the mallards are left in any number. This is because central Illinois is still corn country, and the mechanical picker leaves much of this prime duck food in the fields. But each year the pickers become more efficient and new methods are devised enabling corn to be harvested earlier and dried artificially, and some even maintain that the club that intends to furnish good shooting for its members must violate the law and feed ducks on its own.

Today the state has plans to either buy or condemn large quantities of club lands for public hunting areas. Such areas will allow the man not having or wishing to spend any great amount of time or money to go "duck hunting." And a few of the more lucky hunters will take birds on these public areas so long as a few private clubs remain that control their own rest areas and make sure there is feed available. But if these clubs die, more and more ducks will by-pass this once prime territory.

So today the grandsons try to carry on an ancient heritage by sitting in their blinds to await the "grand passage" that never comes. The grand passage was the big flight — the tremendous flocks of ducks and geese that flew out of the Northland as freezing weather approached. Break of dawn would find flight after flight settling down on the wider parts of rivers and lakes, there to find safety and rest until the vast rafts parted into small groups to find food and shelter. And while early estimates were mostly over-stated, this mass of waterfowl surely ran into the millions.

Back at the beginning of the Golden Age, human populations were small and pollution nil. Duck food along the Illinois was abundant in the form of wild rice, 'coon tail, and the adjacent corn and wheat fields. And at the same time slightly south and east of this area was the vast prairie land of Illinois whose only harvested crop was the prairie chicken. In the 80's, Illinois was still known as the West. Chicago and St. Louis were good-sized towns separated by hinterland. The East

Coast, while populous, centered its people in towns and adjacent farm lands, leaving the coasts, backbays, and salt marshes to the waterfowl.

Even as late as 1900, great bags could be made in the far West where there were few people and little shotgunning was done. Major W. C. Daniels, a Denver millionaire, often journeyed to Utah to shoot the breeding areas and was preceded by several thousand cases of shotgun shells. On one trip of sixteen days, he totaled close to 2,000 ducks. Four men killed 1,493 ducks in two days at Lincoln, Nebraska. E. S. Babcock, of Coronado, California, took 906 one day and 849 the next, and in the San Joaquin Valley, six hunters took 2,700 in six days.

On the opposite coast, W. T. Taylor and his wife, of Trenton, New Jersey, shot the high tide for two and a half hours and killed 500 rail. Carolina hunters were busy taking vast bags of quail, and prairie wagons were being filled with "chickens."

While the amount of game taken was tremendous by today's standards, there is little evidence to suggest it went to waste. And why should it? Anything that couldn't be eaten or given away by the hunter could be sold on the local market, paying for his trip and in most cases showing a profit.

But the sportsman himself was becoming concerned over these large bags. While few suggested that a limit should be placed on what a hunter could take, they did suggest limiting spring and summer shooting. But again, not all were in agreement. As one man wrote, "We see no difference whether a bird is killed in the fall or spring. One killed in the fall cannot return to the nest any more than one killed in the spring."

The state of New York had its first game laws on May 9, 1869. They prohibited the taking of wild pigeons from their nesting grounds and wood ducks, dusky ducks (black ducks), mallards, or teal between February 1 and August 15, except on waters of the Long Island Sound and the Atlantic Ocean. Night shooting and Sunday hunting were also banned, with a fine of $50 for each offense. Some ten years later still found the month of August open in almost all states for legally taking woodcock, plover, snipe, and prairie chickens. This, in spite of the fact that the prairie chicken was not firm of flesh during this period and the young could barely fly.

But state by state enacted prohibitions on either the shooting of game in the spring and summer or sale outside of the state in which

[3]

it was taken. And by 1890 many state game associations had been formed. These were composed of sportsmen themselves with no official standing, and often connected with trapshooting and hunting clubs. Almost all had the avowed purpose of seeking enforcement of existing game laws and enacting new. Wherever game was still being sold in violation of the law, association members would visit hotels and restaurants in committees of two, and when finding game being served would bring suits against the establishment.

What few state laws there were differed on the opening dates of the season, so those states with earlier seasons were overrun with hunters from nearby states which had a later opening date. Most early game laws were full of loopholes and made little sense. Oregon, for instance, passed a law in 1874 that contained a number of prohibitions and then said at the bottom, "Nothing in the above shall be so construed as to prevent anyone from killing any of the above mentioned game for their own use."

Passing a law and enforcing it were two different things, especially when you consider there were only three game wardens for the entire state of Illinois as late as 1887. So most hunters went on their way hunting in the manner and time of their choosing, often unaware that laws existed or were being broken. Game laws were posted on the wall of each post office, but for the most part they were not read, either because the hunter couldn't read or didn't take notice.

The general public attitude was one of unconcern. The farmer shot prairie chickens from his kitchen window whenever the need of his family arose. The sportsman still shot until his ammunition ran out or his means of transportation was loaded with game. The prairie chicken fed in the grass from sunrise to about nine in the morning, then went to corn or tall weeds to remain until late afternoon. It was in these early and late hours that the birds were hunted most because the preferred way of taking prairie chickens was by wagon. Since the birds were not full grown until mid-September, only the market and pot hunter took them during August.

Prior to 1870, the plover was hunted little by sportsmen, but much by professionals for sale on the market. It was plentiful in the extreme, but so were other larger game birds. The shooting wasn't hard and required little gunning skill. The many species of plover offered endless shooting, and when other game became scarce they took their beating.

Lumped under the one designation were many shorebirds, but the two most sought were the black-bellied and golden plover, the golden being the choice of the lot for table use. But the "upland plover" was the real game bird. He was the Bartramian sandpiper, and he was much sought by the sportsman who had proved his gun on targets of lesser ability in flight. The "upland" was never abundant enough to be of real commercial value, for his numbers were nowhere near that of the golden, and other species of plover.

The golden was about the size of a pigeon, a migratory bird that passed through the shooting areas in both spring and fall. They were more a bird of the prairie than a shorebird. They decoyed readily, and a good kill was considered about 100 per day per gun. The hunter found a flyway, then set out six or twelve wooden decoys, supplementing this with wing-tipped birds when possible. These cripples would also call at passing flocks which would decoy in, be shot at, and then turn and decoy again.

Plover calls were sold on the market, but most hunters gave the "wheet-wheet," a sharp whistle with fingers in mouth. Folding tin decoys were popular. These were simply silhouettes of little weight and could be easily stacked when not in use. Some plover specialists had rigs made for their shooting — a two-wheel sulky with only a seat and large box behind to carry game and shells.

It was called the golden plover because of the yellow speckling on the back of head and neck in the spring. But the male was dark in color with white spots on the breast and narrow white-streaked cheeks. The female being gray and slightly smaller than the male. It arrived in the Midwest the first week of April. In the late 70's they came in "wings" as many as 400 or 500 in number. A shorebird by nature, they found resting and roosting spots along streams and rivers, but fed principally on insects and seeds in pastures and prairies. And often among them could be found the curlew, slightly larger than the plover and resembling an overgrown woodcock except for its curved bill. Both were low-flying birds which the hunters were quick to take advantage of by waiting under flyways. Others hunted them on horseback or aboard a buggy, watching where the flocks would settle and then quickly trotting within gun range.

The Bobwhite quail came to the Midwest with the farmer and was hunted in the 70's very much the same as today. Pointing and setter dogs were in vogue, even more so than now, and few men daring to call themselves a sportsman did not possess a dog. The farmer needing windbreaks planted the Osage Orange in long hedges which offered good cover for quail from both their natural enemies, the hawks, and man and his dog. And then as today there were quail specialists — men who had found the way of quail and delighted in it. Because of the work and walking distances involved, and because quail were shot singly, they received little attention from the market hunter unless he was a netter.

Before the setting of seasons, the quail hunters went afield even in August, but found their best shooting, as we do now, in November and December. And nowhere was the sport brought to such a science as by those gentlemen of the Southeast whose income allowed them to make quail hunting a full-time occupation. Throughout Virginia, the Carolinas, and into Georgia a good quail dog brought close to the same price as today. A $500 dog was not common, but there was certainly nothing remarkable in spending that much.

Even though there was no limit set on a day's bag, there were "gentlemen's agreements" and most plantation owners believed twenty-five birds per day enough for anyone. Not so in the far West where it was reported that, "Near the San Antonio and Aransas Pass Railroad in Karnes County, Texas, scores of eighty-five and ninety quail per day are not uncommon, and a man who is unable to count sixty in the bag at the set of sun thinks himself unlucky."

Snipe hunting is now again open to sportsmen in many areas, but it is little followed today. It was very popular prior to this century. But most seasons were closed in the late 20's and did not reopen until near 1950. Consequently, there is a whole new generation of hunters that has never shot snipe or at least is little familiar with it as a game bird.

The nineteenth century hunter ranked snipe right up with the woodcock as a smoothbore target. It was also a mark for the commercial hunter because of its habit of bunching on low tidelands and along the shores. It could be shot in "walks" or "wisps" with as many as ten or twenty birds falling to one shot. The sportsman preferred to walk them up, shooting them singly with small, open-bored guns. The best snipe shooting was in the spring of the year as the snipe is migratory. For singly shot birds, a good bag was considered twenty-five to fifty couples a day, although the Eastern shooter might think a fair day's sport was ten or twenty couples. Small shot such as 10's or 12's was used and it was said a man who could kill two out of four would be accounted a good shot.

A dog was of little use in snipe hunting, even for retrieving, as the birds were usually felled in shallow water or on open beaches. Late in the season when they have become fat and lazy, they will often run before the hunter rather than rise. But the old-timer learned to make a squeak similar to their distress signal and they immediately flushed against the wind in their typical zig-zag flight. They were often hunted by placing one hunter up-wind while the other circled behind them to flush them toward his companion.

All snipe, sandpipers, curlews, avocets, and stilts received attention from the nineteenth century gunner, and were hunted in the same ways. The clapper-rail also received a good deal of attention from hunters on the Eastern Seaboard. From New Jersey to South Carolina, rail shooting was popular through out the 80's and 90's, and especially so with the ladies. It was an easy form of hunting, done in mild weather, and the rail itself flew slowly, making an easy mark. Few considered them good eating when compared with other game birds of the area, but even the novice gunner could brag of his bag. The clapper, along with the larger king-rail, swims about with bobbing head among the salt marshes. Fifteen to seventeen inches in length, they have a slightly curved bill, longer than their head.

They were hunted at high tide when the reeds were low, and the double-ended skiffs, poled with eighteen-foot push paddles, could make their way through. The gunner waited in the bow while the pusher stood, shouting, "mark right" or "mark left," as rail were spotted. Pushers got $2 to $5 per high tide, and in the best-known shooting grounds around Port Elizabeth, New Jersey, were often paid more. Light loads of No. 10 shot were used, and the limit was whatever the shooter could take in some two to three hours. Most were shot on the water as they would more often swim and dive than take flight.

At one time, the wild turkey was plentiful throughout much of the United States. It was said to be so common in the Midwest that slabs of turkey breastmeat were often used for bread due to the scarcity of flour. But it was difficult to hunt, then as well as now, and the fantastically large bags taken on other game never applied to the turkey. It is a bird of the forest, always shy and wary, preferring to run and never taking wing if it can avoid doing so.

They were usually hunted late in the season by their tracks in the snow. And though turkeys were rather numerous in the 70's and 80's, the hunter taking one or two a day thought himself successful. More turkeys were taken by the farmer and homesteader than the sportsman. This was because the birds usually returned to the same roost and could easily be killed after dark by someone familiar with their habits in a given area.

The woodcock is highly spoken of in shotgunning circles, both past and present. There seems to be no principal difference in the way they were hunted, the main difference being in their numbers. Seldom will a woodcock present itself as an open target. It prefers to fly through dense cover around stream beds. Capt. Bogardus remarked that the most he had ever killed in a day was fifteen couple. He said that he had heard men boast of having killed fifty couple a day, but if they did, the birds must have been vastly more abundant than he had ever seen them anywhere. The only method known of taking them in large quantities was that used by Negroes of the southern states. The bird was plentiful along the edges of the bayous at night. Boats and torches were used and it was said that the hunters would paddle along, knocking down woodcock with sticks.

A form of duck hunting peculiar to the Eastern shores was that of the tolling dog. Diving ducks such as canvasbacks, redheads, and bluebills showed a peculiar curiousness about a dog or fox running up and down the beach. Over a period of years, this was taken advantage of by many hunters who trained dogs of any breed from retriever to mongrel cur to trace back and forth, arousing this curiosity and leading the raft of ducks to swim toward shore and within gun range.

It became quite popular during the late 70's and early 80's. While almost unknown today, it was considered a standard form of hunting in many areas then. A description of tolling was printed in the *American Field* in 1881 and is as follows:

> This is the most novel mode of shooting ducks now in vogue, displaying on the one hand the sagacity of the dog and his susceptibility to education, and on the other the engrossing curiosity of the bird. One or more gunners ensconce themselves behind a blind constructed close to the edge of the water. They are accompanied by a dog trained for the purpose. As the morning dawns, the ducks are seen in the distance quietly feeding. The dog now takes his post at the edge of the water and, keeping his eye on the gunner, commences a series of frolicsome gambols, running to and fro on the

[8]

margin of the shore. His limits are prescribed by the sportsman — a wave of the hand or toss of a stone from one side of the blind to the other. If the dog is well trained, he plays in one direction until signaled, then turns and commences his gambols in the other. The curiosity of the ducks is soon aroused and the movements of the dog receive their undivided attention. As they commence swimming nearer, the dog gives no attention whatever to their approach but continues his play until they are within a proper distance when the gunners fire into the deluded flock.

If the dog is not thoroughly trained, he is worse than useless for tolling, for if he stops his play for a moment to look at the approaching ducks, so great is their cautiousness they are instantly alarmed and will alter their direction before getting within gun shot. To make the dog more attractive to them, a red flannel is sometimes bound around the animal.

This natural curiosity of diving ducks was well-known and was often used to draw their attention while in flight to the gunner's spread of decoys. It was common for the duck hunter to tie a white cloth to a stick and when a flight of birds appeared, wave this several times in the air to attract their attention to his stool. Other gunners merely tossed their caps into the air, which probably appeared to the distant ducks as others of their species landing among the decoys.

"Line" shooting was popular along the Atlantic shores, where ten or fifteen boats would form a hunting party. They were distanced two gunshots apart, or so that the mid distance between them would be one gunshot range from either boat. The line of boats would stretch a half mile long, while other power or sailing craft would be upwind driving birds toward the line. It was often a betting proposition with each boat tossing so much in a kitty, to be divided among those boats with the greatest bag at end of day. It was a particularly productive method of shooting coot or mudhen, since these birds seldom flew but a few yards above the water.

Leading and stalking behind a live cow or horse was a common way of approaching cornfield feeding geese, and some stalkers used the hide of an animal thrown over the head and back of two stooped men, giving the birds the impression of a grazing animal. This was the principal method used by the market hunters, who provided the meat for "Pomeranian goose," the breast of swans and geese pickled or smoked. It was quite a delicacy and sold for high prices.

The commercial taking of passenger pigeons is covered in another chapter, but in spite of their abundance prior to the 80's, the passenger pigeon was little sought by the sporting gunner. Those who did usually shot them from stands — these about ten feet high and placed in line with the main body of the flight and near a feeding area. Grain was scattered around the stand and live birds that had been wounded or netted used as decoys. They had a string attached to one leg and were tossed into the air to be pulled back to earth with wings aflutter, and making their call of "keek-keek-keeek."

Some birds were tethered on poles, or "stools." This gave rise to the name "stool pigeon," which has come down to us with slightly different connotations. Flocks of several thousand birds could often be lured to only a few decoys.

Perhaps one reason passenger pigeons were little sought as a sporting bird was because their flesh was considered less desirable than that of most other gamebirds. The usual method of cooking pigeons was in a pie, and the following recipe of 1872 is probably representative:

> Six young birds stuffed with their livers chopped with parsley. Salt, pepper, and add a piece of butter. Cover bottom of baking dish with small slices of beef sprinkled with parsley and mushrooms. Place pigeons on top of this. Between each layer put the yolks of hard-boiled eggs. Scoop brown sauce over the top and cover it with puff pastry. Bake one and a half hours.

Ice shooting was a common late-season method of obtaining wildfowl. Holes were chopped in the ice of shallow bays with the gunners building blinds of block ice, or simply lying under white sheets when there was snow. The ducks readily came to the open water and it was a most productive way of hunting after a big freeze.

The sandhill crane was abundant throughout the Midwest until the late 80's. His body is as large as that of a goose, and his long legs make him four or five feet high. He was considered very much a gamebird then, and he is now in a few areas of the Southwest. In olden days, they fed among the corn much the same as geese and ducks. But they had an advantage in that their bill was more adapted for taking corn off the ear. They were so hard on the farmers' crops that boys were employed to keep them away.

The sandhill is a wary and shy bird with excellent eyesight. While they are hunted over large decoy silhouettes today, it apparently was not a known method of hunting until recently. In times past, these birds were taken by hunters who noted their flights and crossing places as they went to and from the cornfield. In the early fall they flew low and slowly and were easy to hit, but notoriously hard to kill, for they were thickly feathered. No. 1 shot with strong charges of powder was recommended.

The whooping crane (or "white crane" as these were called, along with egrets) was not a field bird and was seldom killed except near ponds where they came to roost nightly. And this was the time that most were taken. But both the whooping crane and sandhill crane were dangerous customers when crippled — said to always aim at the eye with their sharp pointed bills. Dogs were seldom employed in the hunting of cranes as a crippled crane would drive his bill into a dog as if it were a knife.

While never abundant on the market, the crane was shot by the hunter for its fine eating. The meat was dark and the breast was hung to ripen as was the custom of the time. This was then said to equal the best venison. The breasts were large and often cut into slices or steaks, then fried in butter. When possible the bird was frozen and thawed a number of times which made it very tender. In fact, it was said you could hardly hang them too long if the weather was cool, many being eaten a month after they were hung.

In researching the eating habits of our forefathers, one thing becomes readily apparent — our tastes have changed. It would seem that perhaps fifty per cent of the game they ate and relished, we would now throw away as spoiled and contaminated. The cutting of ice from frozen riverbeds occupied as much time as the cutting of the season's wood pile for the average homesteader. This was put in icehouses, usually crude, log, open-topped huts. The ice was cut in blocks with layers of sawdust between. It was usually cut in January or February, placed in the icehouse, and there would be remnants left well into the following winter.

But it was used sparingly and seemed to figure little in the preservation of game. But then, even as today, most "spoiled" game became that way a short time after shooting. This was especially true of the prairie chicken when shot in August or September. The flesh of these birds was not firm during these months even when alive, and they were shot on hot prairies to be piled bird after bird, one atop another in wagons, and perhaps not drawn or plucked until the following day. The body heat of the birds alone was enough to spoil the flesh, to say nothing of the hot sun. It is casually mentioned in many hunt reports that the entire bag was discarded because of spoilage. Research leads me to believe that game had to be pretty rank not to be considered succulent by the hunter of the day.

Domestic meat and fowl was hung outside markets regardless of sun or flys. Game to be kept a considerable length of time was made into spiced meats, especially wursts, where it was smoked, dried, and highly spiced to preserve it. The sportsman was told to smooth the feathers of his downed bird and put a leaf under each wing. This was supposed to help cool the bird and thought by many as a sure preventative to spoilage.

The freshest game was eaten by immigrants. Every Sunday morning throughout the spring, summer, and fall, an army of Italians, Bohemians, and Poles went out of every great city and every large mining town armed with old muskets and cheap shotguns. These men and boys killed everything they could find that flew, including robins, bluejays, and blackbirds. They killed not for sport but for meat, and the birds all went immediately into the pot.

The sportsman of the day had colorful terms of venery for the game he hunted. We find some of these being revived by outdoor writers of today who love to write of a "gaggle" of geese. At the time this term was in common use, geese were only a "gaggle" when on the water; when flying they were called a "string" or a "skein." Turkey were "droves" or "flocks"; grouse a "pack," "brood," or "family"; quail a "bevy" or "covey"; ducks in general were called a "paddling" or "raft" on the water, and a "team" on the wing. According to species, mallards were a "sord"; and widgeon called, according to the numbers, a "pair," a "couple," "bunch," "trip," and "knob"; coots a "covert"; sheldrakes a "dopping"; and brant, a "gang." Swans were a "herd" or "whiteness"; it was a "flight" or "fall" of woodcock; a "wing" or "stand" of plover; a "nide" of pheasants; a "herd" of curlews; snipe, a "walk" or "wisp"; herons and cranes, a "sedge"; wild pigeons, a "flight"; and bay and shorebirds in general, a "flock."

While the East Coast gunner was never far from a well stocked sporting goods dealer, those in what was then the West — Illinois, Indiana, Missouri, etc., and living in other than St. Louis, Chicago, and other large cities, bought their hunting supplies from the general store. While the distances involved between rural and metropolitan areas do not seem large today, it must be remembered that transportation before the turn of the century depended on wagon and railroad. In 1833 there were even few wagon roads through the forests and prairies, and no bridges over the streams of Indiana and Illinois. A trip from Ohio to Illinois at that time lasted a month.

By 1856, the Illinois Central Railroad ran into the city of Kankakee, Illinois for the first time — that city then consisting of one shanty and a blacksmith shop. The whole country south of that point was sparsely settled. And even by 1870, travel from one Midwestern village to another was limited to horseback or by wagon in fair weather only.

So the rural hunter devised much of his own equipment. Standard duck hunting wear prior to the 90's consisted of burlap bags cut with armholes and worn over whatever other clothing the hunter may have had. This was the camouflage suit of the day. Woolen long-johns were a staple item, complete with trapdoor and built-in itch. Over this was thrown a flannel shirt and woolen or cotton pants, although many of the more primitive hunters still wore trousers of buckskin.

The wealthier and more sporting element of the day went in heavily for corduroy in both coats and trousers. Canvas hunting coats, differing little in design or appearance from those bought today, were popular, as was the dog skin coat. This coat differed considerably in quality from garment to garment, but was extremely light, pliable, and warm for leather. The cheaper ones having been made from the hides of several different mongrels. The more expensive showed the slick, glossy coat of a pure bred. This was the day of $.25 a pound beefsteak and $.10 a pound bacon, but a good dog skin coat would set you back $20. One manufacturer had his own island on the Hudson where dogs were turned loose to breed. They were fed twice a week on the contents of a garbage scow.

The duck hunter wore "gum" boots of stiff, black rubber that he often insulated with the breast-down from waterfowl he had taken. Sweaters were in vogue — the heavier the knit, the better, often in turtleneck style and worn under a rubber slicker as much to break the wind as for rain protection.

The waterfowler made his own boat, or bought locally a design that had been found best suited to his area and type of hunting. He did the same with his decoys, and the design of these also varied with the locale. There are forty-eight species of ducks, geese, and swan that fly over North America, and all are decoyable. At one time or another, all have been hunted for feathers or food and taken over stools of decoys. The beginning of decoy-making is lost in antiquity, but we know the early American Indian made use of mud and straw, shaped into rough bird form and set along the banks of rivers. And then he made straw bodies to be covered with the skins of dead water-fowl.

The carved wooden decoy as we know it today appeared before 1800 and slowly evoled into the true art form it achieved by the 1850's through late 1930's. These hand-carved decoys reached a degree of excellence in America that was unique. The designs were of regional nature and the decoy making centers of the East Coast and Midwest were as well-known for the quality of their wares as was Dresden for china, or Sheffield for silver.

Each area produced highly individualistic art. The advanced collector today not only recognizes at a glance the work of a certain region, but often the name of the man carving it. The old-time craftsman painted plumage on his decoys as naturally as his talent would permit. It was meticulously done by fine brush, natural sponge, and a leather comb (usually English-made) to produce a feather-like effect. In the early days, there was little difference between "gunning" and decorative painting. Each maker had his own formula for mixing superbly water-resistant paints. Most of these were linseed oil based, and each man had his own method of "flattening" to avoid glossiness or glare, yet retain the inherent weather-proofing of the oil.

Seasons were long and ran into colder weather than we now experience with our short gunning time. The old-timers made a decoy to take the punishment of high winds and heavy ice. A good handmade "block" was hollow and rode high in the water. The raised head — higher than modern design — was done so for the express purpose of preventing "bill-ice," the weight of which would sink the head end of the decoy giving an unnatural appearance. Our modern theory is that a raised head represents an alerted duck, but the old makers didn't know that and it seems the birds didn't either.

The bread-and-butter ducks have always been the mallard, canvasback, pintail, redhead, and black duck. For this reason, and because they were most numerous, decoys of these five species were in the majority. While the collector will run across an occasional wood duck or widgeon, they are not too common and, except for certain areas, were usually a caprice of the maker to offset the monotony of every-day carving of mallards and canvasbacks.

The extra-large decoys much in favor now were practically unknown. Almost all decoys made before the twentieth century will be found life-size or smaller. White pine was plentiful and used the most for hollow, handmade decoys. They were built by taking two blocks of wood, gluing or screwing them together, and then shaping to a rough outline of a duck body by hand axe, draw knife, or spoke shave. The head was carved individually, then the body was smoothed with rasp, file, or sandpaper. The two blocks were taken apart at the seam and hollowed out as much as possible without weakening the decoy. This gave a full-sized mallard decoy weighing less than one and a half to one and three-quarters pounds.

Early decoys used a deep wooden keel along the bottom. This was later replaced by a flat, lead strip to keep the duck upright and prevent it from bobbing about in rough water. The twine anchor string was preserved by tar for waterproofness, and the anchor weight size and shape depended on the type of bottom found where the decoy would be used. For deep and rough water shooting, this anchor was often of molded lead in whatever shape was found to held best. For shallow bays and calmer waters, everything from rocks to old oarlocks was used.

Live decoys were legal and used for both ducks and geese. These were seldom, if ever, used in great numbers — a dozen being considered a large spread. The norm was four to six calling hens. They were supplemented by many wooden decoys. The small English callers were highly thought of, as two or three of these noisy hens would continuously call to passing ducks.

They were tethered in many ways, often by the duck harness. This was a leather contraption fitting around the body and under the wings, but allowing the duck to stretch, flap, and move about. Most commonly used was a leg strap, usually less than a foot long piece of leather going around the duck's leg and then attached to a line with swivel between. These decoys were furnished with "stools," either a stake or platform where they could occasionally climb out of the water and rest. This was done not so much out of kindness by the hunter, as economic necessity. A tethered duck tended to become wet and chilled and could not long survive icy water.

Around ponds where there was a permanent shooting place, cages of chicken wire were erected and the decoys left loose inside. Some decoys were trained to be flyers. A reel of string was attached to their foot and as a flight of ducks approached, they were tossed into the air to fly out a short way and then to be pulled back and down into the water by the hunter in the blind. To the passing flight of ducks, it appeared only to be another wild duck alighting among the decoys. Stories are often heard of the "free-flight" flyer. This live decoy was supposed to have been trained to fly out to passing flocks of wild ducks and lead them back to the gunner. I have been unable to verify a single instance, but it's a story oft repeated.

According to most reports, wild geese made poor live decoys. These were often wing-tipped birds captured and saved to be staked out among wooden decoys or silhouettes. But it is said that they would only go as far as their leg leash would allow, then huddle down flat against the earth to stay there until picked up by the hunter.

The duck call had its origin in Europe but was not popular there — a fact that is still true today. Duck calling, as we know it, seems to have started along the Mississippi and Illinois Rivers. The first call to become well-known was the "Illinois River Call." It was a pattern, rather than a brand, and made by many hunters for their own use.

Fred Allen, of Macomb, Illinois, was a famous market hunter and part-time inventor. His Allen Duck Call sold widely in both East and West during the early 80's. By 1893 Charles Grubbs, of Chicago, improved the old Illinois River Duck Call and sold a regular model at $.55 with a special model made of red cedar, or a silver mounted one with silver reed, at $1. (This call was obviously a model for the famous call made by Charles Perdew, of Henry, Illinois, although Perdew later changed his calls to all wood and retained the silver mounted models only for his crow call.)

Such were the principal targets, tools and techniques of the bird hunters of the Golden Age, and the hunting conditions. With game plentiful and legislation controlling its harvesting largely non-existent, it is not surprising that the professional bird-hunter had an easy time of it, the life every wing-shot dreams of. Or did he? Let's take a closer look at the profession of market hunting in the next chapter.

[CHAPTER TWO]

The Market Hunter

IN 1918, the market hunter was legislated out of business — but he was through anyway. His period in American history lasted only some forty years, and his ranks were filled with both gentlemen and scoundrels. Nearly all believed game belonged to those who could take it, and the supply to be inexhaustible. The market hunter was a workman of his time, following what he believed to be a legitimate profession.

Prior to the 80's, a man need only look at the fall sky to see that ducks were plentiful enough to feed the whole country forever. And when you tired of eating duck there were prairies full of "chickens" and quail and fat plover. If the head of the family was not a hunter himself, the commercial hunter would see that game was daily fare at prices a man could afford.

There were fifty million Americans in 1880. The center of population was eight miles from Cincinnati. It was estimated that seventeen per cent of Americans didn't know how to read or write, but ninety per cent of the households owned a gun. While this largely rural population could supply much of their own game, the great cities of the East grew greater and game, and land on which to hunt it, was disappearing.

But the people in these cities had in their youth acquired a taste for game. Now the city dweller had more money but less time, so it was natural for him to seek game in the market place rather than the field. This need was filled by a new type of professional — the market hunter. He kept the markets brimming throughout the year, except from mid-June through mid-August when the birds were of such poor quality that no one cared for the taste.

Even at peak prices, prairie chickens and ruffed grouse could be had at $1.25 per brace; ducks at $.50 large and $.25 small; plover and shorebirds at $3.00 a dozen — all tastier, if not cheaper, than the going price for dry-picked chickens at $.18-.22 per pound.

Commercial hunting grew to where the early 80's found over 500 market hunters working at their trade in Currituck County, North Carolina. Wholesale buyers from Baltimore and New York waited on the beach with barrels and ice. There were three or four buyers in the area with one known to have bought over 40,000 ducks a year. Wild celery-fed canvasback had a ready market throughout the East, and the businesslike hunter could take 200 per day, with a few brant thrown in.

The entire East Coast was shot over for market and the same thing was happening in the Illinois and Mississippi River valleys. As in all trades, some commercial hunters were more skillful or better workmen than others. The Chesapeake Bay battery shooter could average between $1,000 and $2,000 a season. But for the average market hunter it was feast or famine. For every successful gunner, there were hundreds who merely supplemented a meager income with what game he could manage to take.

For the most part, the commercial hunter was an uneducated man whose only skill was a knowledge of the out-of-doors. He usually lived on or near the water, and did his forefathers. He fed his bunch of hungry kids by hunting, fishing and trapping, with a few odd jobs in between. As a hypothetical composite of all the professional market hunters of the day, let us consider the life of a man we'll call "Gilly Gerstner."

Gilly would have been more fortunate than many, for he owned a team of horses and a box wagon. This relative wealth was important, for it enabled him to acquire more. A man needed a wagon; after all, ten brace was about all the ducks a man could carry on foot, and he couldn't take them very far. But Gilly could fill his wagon with several hundred ducks and take them quickly to the depot or docks.

A stern-wheeler made a pickup every other Thursday at Bath, Illinois, and would accept his barrels of game, whether "chickens," ducks, or shorebirds. The dockmaster would sign for the shipment and this in turn would be signed by the Chicago buyer, and credited to Gilly's account after freight had been paid and deducted. The buyer always signed that a few barrels were received in bad condition — the game having decomposed and being unsalable. Gilly accepted this as a part of the business and seldom commented on it, to other than a few friends who made a large part of their living in the same way.

He thought himself lucky to have a market of Chicago clubs and hotels which eagerly bought all the game he could supply. His father before him had no such market nor way to ship it. He sold locally and received prices reflecting the glut of game available — often not enough to pay for powder or shot or the sisal to make new nets.

But 1880 was different. The effects of the war were passing and money was easier to come by. Rail transportation was reaching new and farther points. Gilly thought of this and other progress in living since his father had died in the great Yellow Fever epidemic of '78. It had taken 5,000 people in Memphis alone, and reached as far north as Gilly's home in southern Illinois.

And he recalled the old man having told him never to allow friend or enemy to set foot on his marsh because the day would come when more people hunted and there would be less game to hunt. He had told his son that farming was the coming thing, and as the farmer had more boys he would need more land. And the richest land was to be had by draining the swamps. Only those not drained would hold the birds with which to make a living.

The prairie chicken was gone in numbers where a man could make money, and this was true of the plover and pigeon as well. Only the waterfowl was left and it was a fine way to provide for your family. A hunter was free. He answered to no land owner and did not sweat over a harvest while watching myriads of birds swarm in the distance.

The hours were long and the work was hard, but it was a labor of love. Gilly got up before dawn each day but Sunday. Sunday was not a day to hunt. It was the Lord's day and the game was close to Him and it was the only day to give thanks for the abundance He provided during the week. Not all hunters thought along this line, but Gilly was more successful, and he knew this was one of the reasons.

But he thought of problems he had today that his father never knew. Many small things to make a man worry and spend his time unprofitably. Things like the shortage of barrels. There was no nearby cooperage and flour barrels were not easy to come by in the quantity needed. So lately Gilly had been forced to load his wagon with new barrels at the dock as soon as he emptied it of game. They cost as much as $.50 each. At the wholesale price of $.10 a bird, the first layer of ducks went just to pay for the container.

Drop shot was about the same price as always and the black powder that his father had made himself wasn't costly enough to consider. But now Gilly bought his powder from the mills at an added expense. And while he often shot his father's muzzle loading 8 bore, made long ago by Mr. Cassel, his pride and joy was the new breechloading Ainsworth costing over $100 — almost as much as Gilly had in materials for his whole house. When his wife had complained about the expense of the Ainsworth, he had explained that it would pay for itself. He was tired of letting ducks escape while he was loading the muzzle gun and thought he could take another twenty to thirty birds per day with the new breechloader.

Gilly had planned to recover the purchase price, not only on the additional birds, but by building another boat for sale. He was known as one of the best boatwrights in the area. His boats were made to a pattern common to Midwest waterfowlers, being flat-bottomed mud scows, wide in the beam and drawing only a few inches of water. They would slide easily over grass and flag, and were stable enough to shoot from. Two narrow, wooden runners were placed on the bottom of the boat and acted as keels in high wind, but were principally for use on ice when the marsh and rivers froze over.

His boats were about twelve feet in length and wide-planked with a tar and oakum mixture for waterproofing between the joints. The boat was placed in the water for the wood to swell and as long as left there, made a waterproof craft of light weight, highly adapted for its use on shallow, calm waters.

But Gilly also had orders for several dozen wooden decoys from a doctor and a judge who were particularly fond of his artistry. These too were made after a pattern proved best for local waters. For these he received $20 a dozen, even though handmade wooden decoys by other makers of less talent were readily available at $.50 apiece. Live decoys were kept by a few sportsmen, but these were only a few in number (four or five) and used principally for their calling. So they were supplemented by two to six dozen well made wooden decoys.

Gilly Gerstner was a cut above most market hunters in ability and intelligence. The average Midwestern professional hunter was generally referred to by other tradesmen as "river rats." They often came from a family that had a long tradition of supporting themselves only by hunting and fishing. Their pride and temperament would not allow them to take a "job." Steady work at a trade whether by day, week, or month was not their way of life. Not so long as a living could be eked from the outdoors. This tradition and inheritance can even be found today around famous waterfowling areas and this group makes the most excellent of guides and duck club caretakers.

The life of a Mid-West market hunter wasn't easy — he was up before dawn making ready for the day's work. Then, in spite of weather, he was on the marsh putting out two dozen to 200 decoys; then spent the day shooting and retrieving, coming ashore only at dusk or after. His ducks had to be drawn or hung, depending on his custom and market, perhaps packed and iced in barrels, and he then loaded shells by oil lamp for the next day's hunt. If he cared at all for his equipment, water had to be boiled for cleaning the barrels of his gun and then sperm oil applied. He took what sleep he could. The routine was repeated the following morning.

The East Coast money gunner worked as hard, but in different ways. If anything, his life was more dangerous because of the large open water. But his equipment differed in many ways and was adapted to his use.

In the late 70's the Chesapeakers, except for the battery shooters, thought the 10-gauge too small, as the major portion of their shooting was at long range. The 8-gauge was favored and it weighed from fourteen to seventeen pounds, shot seven drams of powder and one and three-quarters ounces of No. 2 or 1 shot, except in early season when No. 4 killed readily. Some few guns weighing twenty pounds carried ten drams of powder, all of them being double-barreled. The single-barrel 8-gauge was popular in the West but seldom used in the East as no advantage was seen to its use. Weight was essential to avoid recoil, and it was thought if there had to be weight, it might as well be in another barrel. Some used single 6-bores up to forty-eight inches in barrel length, taking a No. 4 shell and weighing eighteen to twenty-one pounds. Their usual charge being twelve, sometimes thirteen, drams of black powder with two and a half ounces of shot.

It was principally on the East Coast that punt and swivel guns were used, both before and after being outlawed. Anything that is much larger or smaller than normal attracts attention, and this would seem to account for the belief by many writers that the punt gun was in common use. It was not. Cost alone ruled them out for the vast majority of working hunters.

An English-made punt gun commanded the same price as two or three top grade shotguns. In England, the punt gun was legal and popular, made so by the writings of Hawker and Payne-Gallwey. Both Greener and Holland & Holland made breech-loading punt guns, but I have never been able to find an American breech-loading punter. The large guns were outlawed in most states by the late 60's, or before breechloaders were much in use. So those we find of American manufacture are muzzle loading. The majority of these were not made as true waterfowling punt guns.

During the 50's, sealing was big business in Newfoundland. As the seals were killed off, many of the 1 and 2-gauge sealing guns found their way down to coast and into the hands of New England duck hunters. Most were very long — being as much as eight feet, and originally flintlocks, modified to percussion. Most of these were not mounted on the boat — only rested on the gunwale, with recoil taken on the shoulder by a mass of dried seaweed serving to soften the blow.

The true punt guns weighed around 100 pounds and were often charged with three ounces (not drams) of powder, plus one and a half pounds of shot. When fired they had to be unmounted to be reloaded, or in case of very heavy and long guns, taken ashore. We also read where the recoil of these large guns pushed the boat back in the water for many yards. But figuring the weight of boat, man, and gun, this would seem exaggerated. The American-made punt guns I have examined have been rather crude homemade affairs, no two alike, and of doubtful safety. But there is no doubt the discharge would leave a wide swath of dead and dying ducks when sculled within range of rafting birds.

Battery guns were homemade affairs too. They resembled small, horizontal organ pipes — as many as ten barrels in a row, ranging from 6 to 12-gauge. Usually, the barrels were of ancient muzzleloaders welded together and set so as to cover a wide area when fired. They were loaded individually but arranged by powder train to fire simultaneously.

They were mounted directly on the boat and aimed by pointing the bow toward the target. They were often rope-lashed, the same as punt guns, and often used on quiet, moonlight nights. Then even an oarsman of small ability could paddle within range of resting flocks, and many swans were taken in this manner. The battery gun and night shooting were outlawed along with the punt gun.

In the 80's, the shooting of sitting ducks was not generally looked on as being unsporting. Many of the commercial shooters thought it the *best* way. And the best way of getting within range of rafted waterfowl was by sculling. The scull boat was built low and flat, drawing only a few inches of water. But the sculling oar needed at least two feet of water, so it was a boat for fairly deep bays and lakes. It used only one oar, leather wrapped at the lock for noiselessness, and mounted at the stern, usually in an offset position. The oar was worked back and forth in a sort of figure eight motion which shoved the boat ahead as if pushed from the rear. This worked well only with the wind or on calm water where the boat made only the faintest ripple.

The bow of the boat was camouflaged according to the season. When trimmed with willows, grass, smartweed, or chunks of ice and snow, the boat could silently scull within range of ducks who saw only a floating log, icefloe, or clump of brush. The hunter would lie in the the bottom of the boat, padded with hay, and peer over the cockpit, combing through the camouflage. Once in range, he would empty one gun at the raft on the water then quickly use another as they jumped to take flight. With closely rafted ducks the two guns could often account for twenty to forty birds. Once the dead and cripples were retrived, the hunter would turn his attention to finding another raft of waterfowl.

Sculling became popular in the 70's when the art was learned from Dutch immigrants and, in fact, was often called a "Dutch boat." Over the years it took many forms from plain mud scow to the highly developed Mississippi scull boat. And since sculling was mostly for diving ducks such as canvasbacks, redheads, and bluebills, the Mississippi boat carried wide mounted oar locks and provision for brushing completely around the cockpit combing. This enabled it to be used as a portable blind for mallard shooting in flooded timber.

The "battery" was a watertight, coffin-shaped box just large enough for a man to lie down. It was often called a coffin boat, or just a "float." The box was set in the center of a solid platform, running out some two or three feet on both sides. In the front were large wings hinged to the platform to ride with the waves.

The battery box was ballasted with rocks or sand to water level. Ballast was adjusted according to the weight of the gunner and his equipment. The wings, or fenders, were often ballasted by use of cast iron decoys. These too adjusted according to the height of the waves, as the battery box depended on its hinged outriders to keep seas out of the cockpit.

The battery was anchored with its bow to the wind and decoys put out about it. The box itself was usually made of white pine or cedar, caulked with oakum, and the bottom often padded with straw. Earlier batteries used outriders of boards, but since these were often too heavy, this soon gave way to the use of canvas, painted as near the color of water as possible. It also permitted rolling up the canvas wings for easier towing of the box to its shooting ground.

The battery could only be used in fairly calm weather. Heavy seas made them untenable. The "keeper" boat was used to tow the battery into position and then retired some distance away to act as retriever for the battery. This was a diving duck rig and the usual decoy set consisted of 125 to 200 canvasback or redhead. Often a dozen or more goose or brant decoys were set on the outside edge to act as "confidence" blocks.

The gunner lay on his back in the box with head propped up on a slanting headboard, and from this concealed position could scout about half the horizon.

George Grinnell, in his book, *American Duck Shooting*, tells us,

> Most battery men used guns with thirty-two inch barrels, so that they will be long enough to rest on the footboard. A gun with thirty inch barrels is likely to slip down into the box and so be less easily managed. A good many accidents have occurred by men using guns that were too short, which slipped down into the battery, and, exploding, have shot off their feet.

Decoys were set in such a pattern that ducks would alight directly in front of the battery. In his cramped position, the gunner did not have a wide range of fire. He could shoot only straight ahead and slightly to the front and right, which he did by raising himself to a sitting position.

But the battery was a deadly affair, claimed by at least one authority to have accounted for more canvasback than now exist. Many records exist of a one-man battery taking over 500 ducks per day and 200 to 300 were not thought exceptional. On calm days the keeper boat would sail throughout the bay disturbing the rafted ducks and driving them toward the battery.

Battery shooters were a breed unto themselves and seldom hunted any other way. They often had pots or contests going. One of the most famous shots of the Havre de Grace area was William Dobson. He won a pot of $680 on opening day of 1881 by killing an even 500 canvasbacks.

In 1880, Maryland limited the number of batteries that could be used. They had to be licensed at a cost of $20 for either double or single rigs; and while any amount of sneak or scull boats could be used, there was a license fee of $5.

The East depended principally upon the battery shooter for its supply of celery-fed canvasback. In the 50's this bird was so often fed to slaves that there is history of revolt for this reason alone. But by 1890, Chesapeake canvasback were selling at $7 per pair. This reflected not only the popularity of the bird itself with Eastern gourmets, but also the scarcity of the birds over their previous numbers.

The local population, and even the market hunters themselves, held this bird in high esteem. Throughout Maryland the delicacy was thought by many to be unfit for the table if left in the oven five minutes too long. Great pains were taken in carving. The meat was to be cut with, and not against, the grain. And it was said a good quick oven would cook a full-sized duck in twenty-two minutes. After it was picked and drawn, water never touched it. It was simply wiped dry and the birds were served in pairs in hot, dry dishes — never with a gravy, because, as one hunter remarked, "Immediately they are cut, they will fill the dish with the richest gravy that ever was tasted, and the triangle of meat comprised between the leg and wing with its apex at the back and its base at the breast, is the most delicious morsel of meat that exists." In the hunter's home the canvasback was most often served with hominy fried into large cakes. But the bird could only be eaten this way locally, for the ducks offered for sale to the large city restaurants and homemakers had undergone a change.

The battery shooter hunted from dawn to dusk, piling his birds in the keeper dory. These were brought back to be dumped ashore and sorted, sometimes drawn, sometimes not, then placed in a barrel layered between ice. The less ice, the more ducks could be packed per barrel, and the less the transportation cost. These were shipped by rail, wagon, or steamer to the Eastern point of distribution, there to be drawn and hung by their necks outside the stalls of Eastern meat markets — this to further ripen the bird to the prevailing taste of the day, a taste acquired by some families and handed down until well into the twentieth century. What we would today call decomposed, was then thought "ripe." This gamy flavor could only be partially disguised by long cooking and basting of the birds with burgundy. The Chesapeaker who ventured from home to be "treated" to canvasback was often disgusted by the treatment of his familiar fare.

Ducks were trapped, netted, shot, and taken in every way conceivable to man — all in the name of commerce. In the 70's a particularly vicious method was called "Fire Hunting," which had been learned from the Indians. Men carried torches into shallow bays where swans and geese had bedded down for the night. The glare stupefied the birds to the extent that hunters could wade among them knocking them down with clubs.

Gill nets were strung from bottom to surface and would entrap as many as 500 broadbills in a night's time. One report told of getting the birds drunk on whiskey-soaked corn and wheat so they could be clubbed on the ground. Corn-baited trot lines were often set, and the drowned and bloated birds preferred by some because they were not shot up.

Night hunting was common in the East, but for some reason unpopular to the Western gunner. And in the far West it became the custom of the market hunter to advertise. Vinson F. Davis, of Brigham City, Utah, printed a circular in 1898 saying he could supply game, and listing the evidence of his skill. "I here print my score of last season. I shot fifty-one days, killed 4,220 ducks, averaging eighty-two birds and a fraction per day." L. W. Smith, of Merced, California, advertised in a paper of 1877 that he and his 4-gauge single barrel weighing twenty-two pounds shot 6,380 geese, 5,956 ducks, 367 sand-hill crane, sixty swan, and 847 shorebirds for the Sacramento market between September 15, 1877 and April 21, 1878. If this is to be believed, it may be an all-time record — but not too unusual. Fred Allen, of duck call fame, hunted Boston Bay on the Mississippi River and in twenty days of 1881, he and friend C. W. Scott shipped 3,900 mallards to the Chicago dealers, Bond & Ellsworth; then in another five days shipped 1,289. Allen himself killed 125 mallards in two and a half hours using an E. C. Green 10-gauge double and a 6-gauge single.

Around the San Francisco area farmers complained bitterly of the destruction of their crops by geese, and they welcomed shooters with open arms. Geese were selling in the market for as low as $.25 each. Mallards and canvasback were $2.50 per dozen, and the markets were overflowing. In fact, hundreds of dozens were left over in the dealers' hands each Saturday night. The following Monday these were placed in the hands of pushcart peddlers to be sold as best they could. It was no uncommon sight to see men on the streets loaded down with strings of ducks and quail, crying them for any price they could get.

The price of waterfowl fluctuated with the supply, not the demand. The demand was there, but in some years the ducks were not. And by the mid 80's it became increasingly apparent that the ducks were no longer with us in their former numbers. Now the market hunter was often forced to travel further from home to find game. Some areas became so depleted that the men would take their families and belongings to move to an entirely different area.

Currituck Sound, North Carolina, supplied the bulk of ducks for the Eastern market from 1850–1900. Then the ducks were gone, and these men didn't know how to make a living otherwise. Some went prospecting and found millions of ducks along the Texas coast. And today we find their descendants living in Corpus Christi and the Aransas Pass areas, people whose forefathers were hunters from North Carolina.

But while the waterfowl of our coasts and inland lakes was being shot for sale by men who specialized in this slaughter, the commercial hunter was also busy clearing the prairies of the pinnated grouse. This "prairie chicken" was found in great numbers over a wide area. It stretched from Ohio through Nebraska and from Minnesota to Missouri. And the only equipment needed to make a living off this bird alone was a wagon, a gun, and plenty of ammunition.

An 1888 circular stated,

$25 REWARD. Not strayed or stolen, but running wild on the wheat fields of Kansas. We want 100,000 dozen and no less. Get your gun and go hunting. We pay spot cash for all you can ship us, f.o.b. your station, packed with plenty of ice. Our references Kansas City State Bank, all express companies and railroads. Fourteen years in business enables us to pay more than any other dealer in Kansas City. If anyone sends you a better bid, let us know as we are stayers.

The chicken was so popular in the markets of the Midwest that they were bootlegged well after laws had been passed prohibiting their sale. Even Armour & Co., of Kansas City, bought and sold thousands of prairie chickens and Oklahoma quail, and was fined for so doing after investigation revealed the game was carried on company inventory as eggs.

Large companies such as Armour offered higher prices than local dealers, and thus made excellent targets for the informers. But many well-known hotels throughout the Midwest served prairie chicken on their menus for years after they became illegal commerce. The prairie chicken was not a hard bird to hit. And while most were shot, hundreds of thousands were netted or trapped because they brought a premium price over those that had been shot. The chicken seldom flew over telephone pole height, and only gradually gained altitude from the ground. Long, wide nets were strung across the prairie and the birds driven into them to become entangled.

The fat, golden plover had a ready market but was little hunted because no one had devised a way to take them in volume. They decoyed readily, but were usually shot singly, and could seldom be found bunched so as to be shot in "walks" as were snipe and other shorebirds. And at a going price of $1.50 per dozen, not enough plover could be taken singly to make the expenditure for shot and powder worthwhile. There was even a market for robins and other songbirds that were highly prized by the Italian and Greek immigrants.

But even though they were buying and consuming the birds in quantity, the public was rumbling at the massacre. Yet, very few even considered laws against the selling of game. It was a way of life that had been accepted in America since the Pilgrims had paid the Indians to supply their colonies with game.

The feeling of most was the same as this quote from a letter printed in 1898.

The subject of prohibiting the sale of game to preserve it is too silly and nonsensical to be worthy of any consideration. It would be quite as wise and reasonable to talk about prohibiting the sale of fish from the seas, lakes, rivers, and streams which provide food for thousands of people. Every law-abiding citizen who goes afield for sport and recreation with gun and dog should have the right to dispose of his game as he pleases, by eating it himself, giving it away, or selling it.

We don't know how much was eaten or given away by the hunter, but an 1881 estimate of the sale in wild game at St. Louis alone was placed at $1 million. A single firm there exported to London markets 1,400 dozen quail, 1,400 dozen prairie chickens, 500 dozen wild turkeys, and to the Liverpool merchants 2,000 wild turkeys.

But by now the game was no longer there in the quantities needed. Domestic chickens, ducks, geese, and guinea hens were selling at less money than wildfowl, and in order to make a living the market hunter had to have higher prices. It was simply taking too long for him to make a decent kill.

Even the general public was aware that the birds were no longer abundant. So it was natural for them to condemn the hunter. Little was said or considered that the population had tremendously increased, and that farming was a principal occupation. The prairies had been burned, mowed, and cultivated, and the habitat of the prairie chicken destroyed. The marshes had been drained and planted — marshes that had once given food and refuge to millions of migratory birds.

A new threat had come on the scene — this was the feather hunter. Ladies' hats began to look like walking aviaries. A fashion that started with a few feathers jauntily tucked in the brim gradually progressed to where whole birds were mounted in tandem, fluttering in the breeze. Plumes, the larger the better, festooned the ladies' hats from Pough-keepsie to Pocatello. The feathered hat fad started about 1875. In the beginning the birds were taken mainly by the hunter's gun, but by the 80's the market was too large to fill and everyone, hunter or not, that wanted an extra buck got into the act.

The choicest plumes were from the snowy egret, and unfortunately these were prime only at the nesting season. The adult bird was shot or netted for their "aigrettes," or nuptial plumes, and the young birds left to starve in the nest. Plumes in fine condition sold readily in the 1890's for $32 an ounce, with about four plumes weighing that amount.

The Seminole Indians were paid to go into the Everglades, take whatever plumes and feathers could be had, and bring them to communal dumping grounds.

Nothing that flew was safe. Not every woman could afford egret plumes or birds of paradise, so the bargain basement market was filled with feathers of gulls, herons, cranes — any bird having plumage. In fact, demand for plumage far outran supply, so the ladies took to wearing songbird skins — stuffed, dried, or spread over their bonnets.

Skins and feathers were gathered from all parts of the country to be shipped to New York milliners and a report tells of a hat factory in Wantagh, Long Island that was destroyed by fire. Listed in the loss were 10,000 skins of seagulls, 20,000 wings of other birds, and 10,000 bird heads. The owner, Mr. William Wilson, said he employed men to hunt and skin birds for him, and that his chief hunter had taken 141,000 birds in the season of 1898.

The Audubon Society launched a massive drive for public support to end this slaughter. The famous Prima Donna, Mme. Lilli Lehmann, had been known for her fancy plumed headwear, but she now gave a speech before each performance saying, "I beg you women not to wear birds or feathers on your hats. Every year twenty-five million birds are slaughtered by this terrible folly." Girls' schools passed out forms for everyone to sign, promising not to wear feathers. Sermons were preached in church, and society editors vowed never to give column mention to any woman wearing plumes or feathers. (But this soon gave way to the papers publishing the names and pointing out that Mrs. "So-and-So" had been seen, much to her disgrace, wearing feathers on her hat.) Letters to the editors contained pleas for laws to be passed while there was still a bird left. A famous poem of the time started,

> She devotes her time to missions in the town,
> and she thinks she is good enough to win renown;
> but the birds upon her hat give the lie to all of that,
> as their poor dead bodies waver up and down.

Congress and the Senate were besieged with letters of protest, but it remained for the Hon. John F. Lacey, Congressman from Iowa, to introduce a bill in 1899 known as the "Lacey Act" which prohibited the shipping of wild game, feathers, and skins in interstate commerce. This effectively stopped the wholesale selling and wearing of feathered hats. But not all women went along with it. Some said they saw little difference whether a sportsman killed a quail or they wore the bird on their hat. Others said the gull, tern, egret, ibis, and other birds of plumage were not fit for food anyway, so why not wear them?

The milliners claimed the Lacey Act had nothing to do with their change of fashion. They said it had simply been decided that flowers were now to be worn. However, to the conservationist the Lacey Act was one of the most important ever passed. It authorized the Secretary of Agriculture to spend funds for the reintroduction of birds that had become locally extinct, or were becoming so, in parts of the United States, and to control the importation of foreign wild birds and animals. It prohibited interstate commerce in birds and wild game of any kind killed in violation of local laws.

It was also the first effective step in eliminating the professional hunter. *The Chicago Tribune* said,

> So much alarmed are the game dealers over the new federal law that Chicago dealers who are in the habit of shipping thousands of dollars worth of game East at this season are virtually shipping nothing. Such places as the Waldorf Astoria and similar high-toned hotels in the East have refused to place game on their menus, and the consumption is light.

A wire fence company took a magazine ad stating,

> There are opportunities now to make big money in squab farming. The Lacey Bill has reduced the traffic in quail, grouse, woodcock, and snipe at least seventy-five per cent, and the demand for squab will increase in about the same proportion.

The New York Produce Review was the unofficial house organ of the game dealer. It went all out in opposition to the Lacey Law and attempted to raise a large fund for the purpose of testing its constitutionality. So while objection was made to the bill on the theory that it was intended merely to strike at the millinery, this was not true. It did effectively stop the feather hunter who would go into Georgia with his nets and guns, take birds for feathers in violation of Georgia state laws, and place them aboard public carriers for shipment before the local wardens knew anything was amiss. It also stopped the export of birds and skins such as a single shipment to London in 1898 of 116,490 skins of hummingbirds.

It also stopped the egg hunting business of the Canadian Indians. Gamebird eggs had been shipped by the hundreds of thousands to Eastern U.S. bakeries. The freshness of these eggs was always in doubt. The Indians' test was whether the egg would sink in water, but L. L. Bales wrote in 1896, "If anyone should ask you if an Aleute will eat embryo geese with their whiskers on — just say he will."

Congressman Lacey, thanking the lawmakers in a speech before the House of Representatives, said,

> We have given an awful exhibition of slaughter and destruction which may serve as a warning to all mankind. Let us now give an example of wise conservation of what remains of the gifts of nature. It is late, it is too late as to the wild pigeon; the buffalo is almost a thing of the past, but there still remains much to preserve and we must act earnestly if we would accomplish good results.

Now, laws were rapidly being passed, state by state, setting limits and seasons in which upland gamebirds could be taken. State game commissions were set up and wardens appointed. But the record shows that this action was instigated by the lawmakers only after begging, beseeching, and harassment from sportsmen's groups and interested individuals.

One of the staunchest conservationists of the 80's and 90's was the editor of *Recreation* magazine, G. O. Shields, writing under the name "Coquina." He and his magazine started the League of American Sportsmen, and he himself originated the term "game hog." *Recreation* magazine spent over twenty years at the "roasting" of the game law violators.

The Audubon Society made itself heard through many of its influential members, but most of all it was the sportsmen's clubs, the members of which were hunters, that we must thank for the ultimate passage of laws to protect our game. Many members of these clubs were Senators and Congressmen, and so each year from 1880 on found more and more statutes on the books — some good, some bad, but the effort was being made.

By 1887 we find state laws such as Virginia's which stated, "Waterfowl shall not be killed in the nighttime. Wild geese may be killed either day or night but in no case may lights of any kind be used in shooting." Michigan said, "No trapping or snaring allowed for market. No punt or swivel guns allowed." Pennsylvania closed the duck season between May 1 and September 1, and protected pigeon nestings from firearms in a radius of one-quarter mile of the nesting or roosting place. New Jersey gave a season from September through December on prairie chickens, and protected its plover from January through August. Georgia closed the season on quail from April to October and prohibited fire hunting except on one's own premises.

Few states placed any bag or possession limit, and while these seasons may seem unnecessarily long to us now, it was quite a departure from being open year round. If today we wonder whether they were passed in too limited a degree, or too late, to save our feathered game population, it would probably be better to reflect that we had gained twenty-six million population, over fifty per cent gain, in two decades, and that much of this was a rural population, hungry to put more land to the plow, to drain more marsh areas, and to build more roads. In any event, the wilderness was disappearing, and along with it the habitat of the gamebird.

The day of large scale market hunting was over in the early 1900's, even though it was legal to sell waterfowl some eighteen years beyond that. A federal law in 1913 would have prohibited market hunting for ducks and geese, but was declared unconstitutional. In 1916 we entered into a treaty with Canada to protect these species, but it was unenforceable as written and the slaughter went on. It wasn't until 1918 that an "enabling act" was passed referring to the sale of waterfowl. But it was another two years before the Supreme Court gave its approval and enforcement began. So the market hunter turned to guiding, boat building, or decoy making for the increasing number of "sport" hunters who would never know the "good old days."

[CHAPTER THREE]

The Pigeon Match

BUT the hunting for wild game was not the only shotgunning sport in the Golden Age. The shooting of trapped and released birds was another favorite activity. Box-birds, flyers, live birds — whatever name you call it — pigeon shooting has always been the aristocrat of shotgun sports. Today, it's where many big-league trap and skeet champions end up after collecting all the titles and silver they desire.

It's still a big money game — both here and abroad — and some European gun handlers make a good living from it. Although legal in many states, matches here are held clandestinely to avoid offending the bird-lover and pigeon-fancier. So it is a "silent sport." Little publicity is given, or wanted. In Europe, most especially Spain and Italy, palace-type clubhouses are built, and shooting is popular with high society. There, the target is a Spanish pigeon — the *"Zurito,"* a small and fast blue-gray bird, often sized through a metal ring for uniformity before being accepted. It has little in common with our domestic pigeon which is lumbering and slow in comparison.

Competitive pigeon shooting today is fairly simple. At the big matches you place your pigeon-chip (a coin-shaped affair) in an auto-matic selector — an electronic machine that unbeknown to you chooses one of five traps which will release your bird. These traps are small metal boxes set in a row, a few yards apart. Now, you step out to the firing line and load your gun. You say to the pull-boy, "*Listo*," or "ready." He repeats it and then holds a sensitive microphone under your arm. From here on, don't burp, sneeze, or breathe too hard. The first noise you make, whether a cough or call for the bird, releases the trap. As the metal sides of the trap collapse, the bird bounds up and away and you have two shots and seventeen and a half yards before he reaches a three-foot high fence that surrounds the pigeon ring. You must kill the bird so that it drops inside this fence. It matters not that it may have been stone-dead in the air and sailed, or was blown, over the fence — it's a lost bird.

The game has changed remarkably little since its beginning, and it is the forefather of modern trapshooting. While there are no authen-tic records as to the exact date of its origin, we are pretty safe in say-ing it started in England around the mid-point of the eighteenth century. The February 1793 issue of the British publication, *The Sporting Magazine*, remarked, "The sport of pigeon-match shooting is common in all parts of England, but none so fashionably followed as in and around London." Since rules of that olden day were much the same as used now, and must have taken many years of trial and error to devise, we can assume the game pre-dated the quote by a consider-able length of time.

And all we can do is assume. Earlier history is even more clouded. Some accounts would indicate the periwigged gentlemen of the day would sharpen their eye and flintlocks on trapped and released wood pigeons as practice for "side" matches regularly held across the chan-nel. These contests on driven game were for large sums, and larger bags. One such match reported that teams of six Englishmen and six Frenchmen took 2,200 birds in three days' shooting, and 10,000 pounds sterling stayed in France.

This may have pushed the British losers toward more practice on live birds and probably evolved into the "help-ale" and "make-feast" matches promoted by enterprising landlords of early English inns. They posted offers of, "Three pieces of plate to be given the three best shots." The birds were released from the hands of lads recruited for the purpose, and if boundaries were used, there is no mention of them. Matches of this nature find their counterpart today in rural taverns with a trap or two out back.

In his book, *The Gun*, Greener tells us the first *bona-fide* pigeon club was the Hornsey Wood House, and this may be so, depending on his meaning of *"bona-fide."* But we know clubs began to form shortly after 1800 and the first of note were "Old Hats," "Red House," and then "Hornsey Wood." The Old Hats, a public house on Uxbridge Road, is commonly given the nod as being first, and derived its name from the practice of placing pigeons in ground holes and covering them with old tophats until released.

The Old Hats soon lost favor to the Red House club which was more conveniently located to London. By this time, rules were formalized, and the birds trapped (released) in much the same way as today. An interesting report of a match held at Red House is to be found in the 1850 edition of Blane's *Encyclopedia of Rural Sports*. It reads in part:

> The zealots in pigeon shooting, of which there are many among the wealthy and influential, are loud in praise of this sport and consider it as the perfection of the art of shooting flying.
>
> A match thus made, several dozens of pigeons having been provided for the purpose are disposed in baskets behind the company, there to wait the destructive crisis.
>
> A shallow box about a foot long and eight to ten inches wide, is sunk in the ground parallel with the surface and just twenty-one yards from the foot-mark where the gunner takes aim.
>
> The box has a sliding lid to which is affixed a string held by one appointed to that office and who on word of command from the gunner will release the pigeon. The gunner is not permitted to raise his gun until the bird is on the wing. The bird must fall within one hundred yards of the box or it is deemed a lost shot.

These first traps were of wood, but Battersea and Hornsey Clubs started using iron. On being pulled, the noisy metal startled the bird into flight. The trap was twelve inches by ten inches and raised three inches off the ground. The four sides of the trap were hinged and the front side was drilled with three holes to admit light. The bird would face the light and always have its tail toward the shooter.

The target had now changed from the wood pigeon to the faster, smaller, and unpredictable Blue Rock pigeon, a chalk cliff nester flying about forty-five mph. If this breed was in short supply the next choice was a domestic variety — the Lincolnshire Blue Rock, which never really became tame and along with a Belgian variety remained the prime British target until 1916 when pigeon shooting was outlawed under the World War I Defense of The Realm Act. It was thought pigeons were being used to carry dispatch notes across the English Channel giving "aid and comfort" to the enemy. The ban was a blow from which English pigeon shooting never recovered.

Sometime before 1831 pigeon shooting made its way to America, and our first records tell of a match held at the Sportsmen's Club of Cincinnati in that year. Within the decade a great many Eastern clubs had been formed and pigeon shooting now became "trapshooting" in America. The target of the day was the then abundant passenger pigeon.

Communications were few and slow in the early 80's so we will never have an accurate estimate of our passenger pigeon population. But it must have been incredible! Reports of the time tell of bands of birds several miles wide, and taking many hours to pass a given point during their migratory flight. The birds were so numerous, and in such demand for both meat and trapshooting, that professional pigeon trappers appeared on the scene. Each club had its favorite pigeon purveyor, and he was often listed by name on the program. His worth was judged by the average of strong, darting birds he could supply at a premium price of $1.20 to $2.40 per dozen. Shipments of young, or sickly, birds were priced after bargaining, and used for practice — seldom in tournaments. During the early 70's there were often twelve to twenty thousand birds in coops at St. Louis or Cincinnati.

Shooting rules were loose and made with more adaptation to the club's physical limits than to uniformity. Larger tournaments tried following as closely as possible the Hurlingham rules[1] with an eighty yard boundary. Some clubs built the low boundary fence, while others used only markers.

Shoots were held throughout the country in towns and villages, but since travel of any distance was by train, the site of larger meets was near a rail center. A few of the tournaments were on 100 birds, but most programs were for seven, ten, fifteen, or twenty at most. Scores of top men, such as Bogardus, ran an average of eighty-seven

---

1 See Appendix C.

kills out of 100, while the less talented could walk away with a lesser title on seventy-five out of 100. But even here, entry fees and purse money were large.

Most matches between two opponents were shot from H & T traps. This simply meant "heads" and "tails," and a coin was tossed to determine from which of two traps the bird was to come. Five traps in a row were not common until late in the 80's.

Ground traps were commonly used, but in 1876 the "plunge" trap was introduced with the favored brand made by W. F. Parker, West Meriden, Conn. They sold for $15 per pair and were made of sheet metal in pyramidal shape, and were set on posts about two and a half feet above the ground. Spring traps were used then, as now, the bird being placed on a spring arm that would toss him straight into the air on release.

Skulduggery was rampant. Boys loading the traps were not above suspicion and were watched carefully. They could squeeze or break a rib cage on a bird to slow him down and favor a certain shooter. Rules often stated that opponents would load and trap for each other and this to be done in common view, preventing them from tearing out a few tail feathers so that the bird would fly erratically.

But wild pigeons were becoming scarce. Fewer shoots were being held on fewer pigeons and for larger awards. The Convention of the New York State Association in 1881 was held on only fifteen birds per shooter, yet it was for a diamond medal claimed to be worth over $1,000, plus large awards of cash and other prizes.

And now shoot reports were beginning to say, as did one, "The pigeons for tame ones, were in the main, strong, good flyers. We could not obtain wild birds." Netters were out as usual, but having a hard time finding birds in the amount required. By train or wagon they carried their collapsible pens, folded for the trip. Most were never erected.

By 1882 it became so bad that many shoots were canceled due to lack of birds. In July of that year one sporting magazine commented,

> The scarcity of wild pigeons this season, it being impossible to obtain them except for larger tournaments, has caused shooters to turn their attention to substitutes to obtain wing practice. In this connection, the flying clay pigeon patented by Mr. Ligowsky is attracting a great deal of attention.

Letters to the magazine asked, "Please tell me where the wild pigeons are this fall." Answer: "We cannot give the desired information. Quite a number of dealers in wild pigeons have had men out in every direction in search of them, but up to the present time without avail."

Since the people were used to seeing what has been described as billions of birds each migration, this sudden scarcity was startling. Leffingwell tells us something of their numbers in his book, *Shooting on Upland, Marsh and Stream,*

> About three in the afternoon flocks of three to five hundred started to fly by. Many flocks were only of males and some of females. The sky was cloudless and the setting sun cast its mellow rays on the purple heads, the blue backs and necks, the golden orange, the cinnamon and copper of their breasts. The main body of the flight started at four o'clock and the flock was fully 100 yards wide and densely massed together. Five o'clock, and then six, passed and still no end to the flight — it increased if anything.
>
> I loaded and fired until my ammunition was expended, and I stood my gun against a tree and silently gazed in astonishment at the wonderful sight before me. And I intended waiting until the last of the caravan had passed. The day grew to a close and the sun sank to rest. Yet the flight never ceased. It was now dark, and the birds could no longer be seen, but the whistling of their wings could be plainly heard.

Many reports of their abundance are given in the works of Audubon and Wilson. And it was said they gathered at feeding places and appeared at a distance like great rolling billows of clouds of blue and white. In 1878 a gigantic roost was located at Petoskey, Michigan. It covered some forty miles in length and varied by three to ten miles in width. In the town itself, the "pigeoners" arrived some 500 strong and set up camp in very hotel and boardinghouse available. All talk was of pigeons and market quotations. The railroad freight house was filled with nets and tools of the trade.

An eyewitness report of the nesting area said, "Every bough was bending under the weight of from five to fifty nests per tree." Local Indians chopped them down and as soon as the fledgling birds were hauled out of the nests, their heads were jerked off and the bodies tossed in heaps to await the wagons. Every farmer in the area was hired with team and wagon to haul dead birds at $4 per wagonload to the railroad, there being some fifty teams in all.

Regular rail shipments started on March 22 and lasted until August 12. Dead birds were packed about 500 to the barrel, and live birds were six dozen to the crate, making a total for this period from Petoskey alone of over 1,600,000 birds.

In 1881 the following appeared in the *New York Sun*:

There arrived on Saturday night at a place near Jersey City a car containing 8,500 wild pigeons that had been shipped from Atoka Indian Territory. They are the first installment of 20,000 which W. T. Thomas, of Phillipsburg, N. J., contracted to supply to the New York State Sportsmen's Association. The pigeons were placed in pens, made of slatted framework, from which they will be taken as wanted. Mr. Thomas makes a business of trapping pigeons for field sport. He will get four more carloads from Indian Territory, making a total of 40,000 pigeons.

He said, "The business will not be a profitable one this year because we have to go so far to get them. Owing to the late, cold spring the birds did not roost as far north as usual this year, but we found them in the Pottawattomie Reservation which is 110 miles from the nearest railroad station. I had to transport all my traps and supplies to the roost and the pigeons had to be hauled back for shipment. At one time I had fifteen wagons on the road and it took a wagon about three days to make the trip from the roost to the railroad. But the roost is the largest I have ever seen. It is post oak timber and acorns are abundant. So it is a splendid feeding ground. I went into the roost for about ten miles without finding any sign of an end. Every tree was thick with pigeons, the branches bending under their weight.

"When the birds come home from the feeding ground in late evening I have seen a stream about a mile broad flow through the air for about two hours, thick enough to hide the sun and making a noise like thunder. I should judge the roost to be about twenty miles long and fifteen broad. There has been little or no shooting so the birds are not scary, and easy to trap.

"The Indians do not care for pigeons so they do not hunt in the roost, but they are very friendly and many of them work for St. Louis firms catching squabs for market. Men go about with poles pushing the squabs out of their nests. They are packed in barrels with ice and sent to all large cities as far north as Boston.

"My business was altogether with live pigeons which we caught in traps or nets. The nets used will cover a space of forty feet by thirty feet. One end of the net is fastened to a rope which is drawn taut so that when let go the net is thrown out falling on pigeons gathered in front of it. They are generally caught on feeding grounds or water beds. When a good feeding ground is located the nets are set and the trapper hides himself in a hut of boughs. Some pigeons are saved as decoys so that when a flock is seen coming, a few birds are thrown into the air to attract attention and then pulled down again with a string.

"I once caught sixty-seven dozen at one cast of the net, but thirty or forty dozen is an average big catch. Sometimes there will only be a dozen or so. I have seen the net lifted on the wings of pigeons until it bellied out like a balloon. A number of birds toward the edge are apt to get out, but the men are quick and work around the edges stocking the birds in crates as fast as they get them out and rolling the net up as they work.

"Early in the morning the tom flight occurs. This is composed of the male birds on their way to the feeding grounds. When they have fed and drunk they return to the nests and the female birds go to feed. The hen flight takes place between eight and nine o'clock. In the afternoon there is another tom flight, and toward evening another hen flight.

"The crates in which the birds are put are simply large flat coops. Every evening the teams take a round and collect all the crates and it is now necessary to get the birds on their feed or else they will die. They are put in pens and given corn to eat with plenty of water to drink. For several days after they are captured they will hardly eat at all and it is only after they have become accustomed to the change that they can be shipped. Two men travel in the railroad car and the pigeons are regularly fed and watered.

"Pigeons nest four times a season having one egg to a nest. The number of squabs killed and pigeons netted is insignificant in comparison with the number hatching out."

In spite of this vast inhumane slaughter by man, it was known that still millions of birds had escaped, and much concern was felt about their whereabouts.

A Chicago newspaper reported,

The winter of 1880–81 has passed into history as one of the severest known in this country. The memory of the oldest inhabitant, often the backer of traditional tales of severe winters and heavy falls of snow, has been unable to recall a season of parallel severity.

This severity has been general throughout our vast territory. From the South, where winter, heretofore, has been a season of pleasure, came reports of deep snows, cold days and nights, and chilling rains. In the Far West and Northwest came tales of fifty degrees below zero. Great anxiety has been felt for the effect on feathered game.

And it was in this following spring the passenger pigeon did not return to roost, except for small and scattered flocks. Rumors spread. Some said they had become confused during a storm and had gone to South America. Many claimed they gathered in a vast flock on the Eastern seaboard and were swept out to sea by a great storm. A ship's captain reported millions of floating dead birds on the Atlantic. Others thought the pigeons had perished from an infectious disease.

By 1886 some bird authorities claimed they were extinct in the wild state. However, it was remarked in *The Sportsmen's Journal* of December 17, 1887, "1,000 wild pigeons are in coop in St. Louis. A few years ago such a fact would not be worth noticing as there were often fourteen or fifteen thousand at a time. But now 1,000 in captivity is so rare that it assumes importance."

Sightings were in vogue and reported to the newspapers. After six years of scarcity, it seems the pigeons were making a comeback in 1888–89. Here are excerpts from *Recreation* magazine in those years:

> For fourteen years the passenger pigeon had thought to be ex-
> tinct, but about the middle of April (1888) the people of Lime
> Ridge, Wisconsin were treated to a sight that recalled the spring
> days of twenty years ago. A flock of wild pigeons passed going
> north and were so numerous that the first flight were out of sight
> before the last had passed. All that seen them were positive they
> were the old-time pigeon.

Another report of 1898 by a reliable source was reported, "A Mr. Ludwig Kumlien, Department of Biology, Milton College, said, 'I think I have seen more (passenger) pigeons during 1898 than from 1890 to this year.'"

"There is no doubt that these birds have appeared at their old stamping grounds in their former numbers and the theories they were extinct seem disproved," said a Mr. Fredrick Wahl, of Milwaukee.

Other reports of that period told of a flock of 1,000 seen near White Fish Bay, and over 200,000 at Black River Falls, and people said the roost was just as it used to be. Evidently the people of central Wisconsin saw passenger pigeons long after they were thought by many to have been gone, but where did they go again?

Recreation magazine published a letter of March 3, 1899 from F. Everett Hall, of Lacona, New York:

> We all remember how we used to look forward to the spring
> flight of pigeons some twenty-five or thirty years ago, and what

thousands of them used to pass over all parts of New York. This town was once a famous feeding ground for them.

A Mr. Miles Blodgett made a business of trapping them for market. One spring in the 70's he captured 3,000 dozen. Once in the spring the pigeons flew north to this part of the state about the last of March, as it set in quite warm. Immediately after their arrival it turned cold and they all disappeared going south.

Mr. Blodgett went south in the state to ascertain if possible their whereabouts and finally located them near the village of Byetown on the New York & Pennsylvania railroad line. Meantimes, the snow had fallen quite deeply and the birds having roosted in small timbers, chilled and would fall out of their nests into the snow. The ground was literally covered and thousands died this way.

Still the main body of the flight had left Byetown going northeast in a storm of rain and sleet. Mr. Blodgett went after them taking the train for Malone. Here he saw small flocks of five or six dozen flying around in a bewildered manner. He spoke of his business and inquired what was the matter with the birds. Some Adirondack hunters told him they had been on the mountain called Two Indians and when coming down had seen at a distance several acres of ground which had a strange appearance.

There was at the time, fourteen inches of snow on the ground softening from a thaw. On reaching the place, they found millions of dozens of dead pigeons, the sleet having frozen on them in flight weighing them down so they fell and died. These men told of walking three miles over dead bodies of millions of birds and later investigation proved the truth of their statement.

The last known passenger pigeon died in 1914 in a Cincinnati zoo. What really happened to them will no doubt remain one of the great mysteries of nature. But they had lost their habitat. Where they had once been widespread into many family groups, the Eastern hardwood forests had been cut over concentrating their nesting and roosting grounds. They had only the Midwest to nest in their usual way, and as farming increased, their forests became smaller.

True, the hunter and trapshooter played no small part in their annihilation, but it would appear that nature herself may have signed the final papers of extermination. From 1887 on it was impossible to obtain wild birds. Trapshooting was carried on to some extent with domestic pigeons, but it was now the wide variety of inanimate targets, invented to replace the now extinct passenger pigeon, which was to become the next major story of the Golden Age.

CHAPTER FOUR

Targets of Transition

WHILE the passenger pigeon was abundant throughout the 1870's and widely used in live-bird matches, it was still a comparatively expensive target, especially for practice. Even the domestic or barnyard variety of pigeon was expensive because of the work in trapping or raising them, and the cost of coopage. It was also a poor substitute for the wild bird as it was slower, larger, and steadier in flight, but could carry a lot of lead.

Blackbirds were tried and proved too easy, while purple martins were too hard to hit and in small supply. Starlings and sparrows were used with some success but could never be trapped in the numbers needed. California began shooting bats. The bat was a target worthy of the finest shots and not a little discouraging to those of lesser ability. Bats were thrown by hand in much the same way as *colombaire*-style pigeon shooting is practiced today in Mexico. But only certain parts of the country could produce enough bats. Around 1880 the fad had worked its way eastward to Louisiana, and bats were shipped from New Orleans to Cincinnati and other areas. While some shooters became enamored, others wanted nothing to do with the sport. One shoot account reported, "As bats are very uncertain property, many of our best shots did not show up."

Since there was little in the way of live targets that had not been tried, the search was on for an inanimate target that could be stored without loss and brought into play only when needed. It was with this thought in mind, we assume, that Boston's Charlie Portlock brought back with him from England the first trap and glass balls to reach our shores. He must have found the English gentry using glass to a small extent and could see greater possibilities for its use by our own shooters.

So far as I can find, there are no records or written history that tell us anything further about Mr. Portlock. There are offhand mentions that could tie Sylvester Roper, his financial backer, Charles Billings, and Christopher Spencer (later of pump gun fame) to Portlock, but nothing definite has been established. The relationship is not clear, but if I were to make a supposition it would be that the first trap was set up at the Roper factory in Amherst, Mass. And an educated guess would be that the first glass ball shoot was held at Boston's Beacon Park in 1867.

But the English trap left much to be desired. It tossed the ball almost straight up, or if tipped to throw horizontally it could only move the ball eight or ten yards in a wide trajectory. This slow moving target was small challenge to trap shooters used to live birds. Yankee ingenuity then went to work and great improvements were made in short time. But it was nearly a decade before glass ball shooting came into prominence. By then, features of the original English trap could no longer be noted in the American models.

The first American patent on a ball trap was in 1876, obtained by Ira Paine, the noted shooter. It was an elastic cord type, clumsy to operate, and never popular. Shortly, trap inventions were flooding the patent office — seven of them in 1877, and one among these was that of Capt. Adam H. Bogardus. It was a simple trap that would throw a ball as far as thirty-five yards. It was light in weight, uncomplicated, and inexpensive ($6.00). The shooters were delighted.

It quickly became *the* trap. Not only had Bogardus invented it, but he could better all comers at breaking the balls it threw. His knowledge, skill, and forceful personality were such that even though John Mole's rotary ball trap, patented only nine months after Bogardus', was perhaps a better, more workable mechanism, it never achieved success with the shooters.

It was also Bogardus who originated the first simple rules of glass ball shooting. They were, all matches to be shot over three traps placed ten yards apart and numbered 1, 2, and 3 from left to right. No. 1 trap threw a left angle; No. 2, a straightaway; and No. 3, a right-angle bird. The gun butt was to remain in a below-the-hip position until after the call of, "Pull!" The size of shot and amount of powder were shooter's choice, but shot was limited to one and a quarter ounces. The yardage was eighteen, with shoot-offs to be at twenty-one. Later, it was added that the ball should be thrown at least sixty feet, and 12-gauge guns were to be given a three-yard handicap over 10-gauge.

In spite of the popularity of the Bogardus trap, which had now become standard at most shoots, Milton Card, of Cazenovia, New York, brought out the Card Rotary Trap in 1879. This met with instant success because the rotary motion imparted to the trap in pulling it off prevented both shooter and puller from knowing which direction the ball would take.

The Stock trap became popular in the Midwest at about the same time. This was the combined ideas of Charles Stock and Fred Kimble. It was manufactured in the back of Stock's gunshop in Peoria, Illinois. Stock's was a hangout for most of the local hunters, and a frequent visitor around the potbellied stove was Frederick Damm who was later to work for the Chamberlin Target Co.

Damm had made several suggestions later included in the Stock trap, and by 1884 had obtained a patent on a trap of his own design that could throw both balls and clay targets. This trap incorporated the basic features and was the forerunner of the famous Expert trap as made by Chamberlin, and later Remington.

D. H. Eaton in his book, *Trapshooting — The Patriotic Sport*, published in 1918, lists thirty-nine patents taken on ball traps between 1876 and 1912. Of these thirty-nine, nine were invented within a fifty-mile radius of Peoria, and most of these ideas can be traced to the trap devised by Stock and Kimble. However, a great many ball traps were in use that the inventor had failed to patent. They all had to be fed, and supplying the demand meant a booming twenty years for the American glass industry.

I have never found a description of the original English-made balls brought over by Mr. Portlock. However, the British ball in use at that time was of hand-blown, clear glass about two and a half inches in diameter. Our American-made balls were standardized to this same dimension and remained so throughout their period of manufacture.

But clear glass was hard to see under many conditions of light and background. They were soon replaced by those made of blue, green, and amber glass. Another problem was that of light reflection, and even worse, the ricocheting of shot from the hard, smooth surface. This led to first coating the balls with sand and later making them of corrugated glass.

One of the first companies to supply glass balls in quantity was Whitall, Tatum & Co., glass manufacturers at 410 Race Street, Philadelphia, and 46 Barclay Street, New York. Their plain, clear glass ball sold for $3 per barrel of 300 balls. They soon replaced these with blue and amber balls and a new claim to regularity in thickness. They also offered their own patented sanded trap balls and noted in their advertisements there was no charge for barrels or drayage.

The sole manufacturer of the Bogardus patented rough ball was J. Palmer O'Neil & Co., of 68 Fifth Avenue, Pittsburgh, Pennsylvania. A free scorebook was packed in each barrel, and in 1881 they sold for $11 per thousand with $.10 per barrel added to cover cost of drayage. This firm also made plain glass balls selling for only $.50 per thousand less.

Henry Sears & Co., of Chicago, manufactured a great many balls under their own name, and sold also to Hartley & Graham; Schoverling, Daly & Gales; E. K. Tryon & Co.; Isaac Walker Hardware; and Hibbard, Spencer, Bartlett & Co. So far as can be determined they were plain glass balls without marking. Those marked with the house brand of the above firms were most likely made by Bohemian Glass Works, 214 Pearl, New York, or Whitall, Tatum & Co.

The Target Ball and Ball Pigeon Co., of Lockport, New York, offered both plain and colored balls for $6 per thousand. They were of uniform thickness and well molded, but the neck section was so thin that complaints of breakage were numerous and they were soon discontinued. Breakage was a large problem, not only in shipping and handling, but in the immense piles of glass collected on the shooting field to endanger barefoot trap boy and shooter alike.

One inventive genius sought the answer in a composition ball, advertised as dissolving into an excellent fertilizer. Other firms made balls of pottery clay, but they were either too hard to be broken, or

Long seasons and large limits (when there were any at all), and the leisure time to enjoy them—these key elements of the Golden Age of Shotgunning seem somehow exemplified by the unknown wildfowler above.

Game was so abundant and bags so large in the 1880's that transport was often a problem for the hunter. The advent of automobiles after the turn of the century finally eased matters.

ERICKSON STUDIO

Danz' New Pat. Decoy Duck

This is a double-facing decoy, consisting of two metal profiles precisely alike, hinged to either side of a flat wooden float. One of these acts as a keel, to hold the decoy upright, but if a gust tips it over, it rights itself and does not turn turtle.

We also make to order the double decoy, with different positions on opposite sides of the float, say a mallard on one side and turkey back on the other, so you have two dozen ducks for the price of one dozen.

Sportsmen who have tried this pronounce it "The Decoy of the Future." Its excellence is so apparent we now make no other style. A large variety always on hand, including Mallard, Teal, Red Head, Canvas Back, Blue Bill, etc.

PROFILE GEESE AND COMBINED ALWAYS IN STOCK

— o —

PRICE LIST:

Duck, either style with cord and anchor, complete............per doz. $12.00
Geese, for stubble shooting................................ " " 12.00
Geese, combined for land or water shooting................. " " 24.00

Fifteen per cent. discount where our goods are not on sale.

For Circulars and Terms to Dealers, address

HORNE & DANZ,

Sole Manufacturers.   ST. PAUL, MINN.

PATENT FOLDING TIN
"PLOVER" & "SNIPE" DECOYS.

Most Portable
and
Best Decoys
Made.

These decoys are made of two oval-shaped parts or sections, which, when closed together, make the exact form of the bird. They pack or nest one into another, so that a box containing one dozen measures only 10 in. by 8 in., and 2½ in. deep; are nicely painted to represent the bird.

Varieties made: Black-breasted Plover, Green Plover, Red-breasted Plover, Turnstone or Chicken Plover and Yellowleg Snipe.

Prices for Plover, $4 per doz. Yellowleg, $4.50. Discount to the trade. Ask your dealer for them.

Golden and Green Plover.

WM. READ & SONS, 107 Washington St., Boston.

Dealers in Fine Guns and Shooting Tackle.

Many varieties of home-made and manufactured decoys were produced during the Golden Age, and these were often supplemented by tethered live birds, which were legal. Legal, too, were battery guns, like the crude, "organ pipe" guns opposite; these were capable of wreaking great destruction on rafting ducks when used from coffin-boats or sink-boxes.

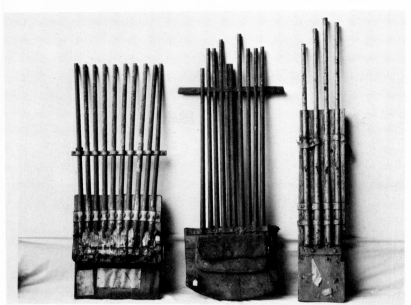

GRAND
SHOOTING TOURNAMENT
AT
BEACON PARK
BOSTON,
UNDER THE AUSPICES OF THE
TREMONT SHOOTING CLUB,
ON
THURSDAY & FRIDAY, Oct. 22 & 23, '74
OPEN TO ALL SHOOTERS IN NEW ENGLAND.

FIRST DAY, THURSDAY, OCT. 22, 1874.

CLASS SHOOTING   Wild Birds   10 Single Birds.   Prizes $150. $10 Entrance.   Divided equally amongst five classes, $30 each

SWEEPSTAKE, $100.   10 per cent. Entrance.

Open to all comers in New England   Wild Birds.   Plunge Traps.   10 Single Birds.   8 Entries to all
First Prize, $50.   Second Prize, $30.   Third Prize, $20.

SWEEPSTAKE. DOUBLE BIRDS.

$100   10 per cent entrance   Purse to fill   Plunge Traps   Five Double Birds   First Prize $50
Second Prize, $30   Third Prize, $20

SECOND DAY, FRIDAY, OCT. 23, 1874.

CLASS SHOOTING   Tame Birds   10 Single Birds   Prizes $150 $10 Entrance.   Divided equally amongst five classes $30 each.

SWEEPSTAKE. DOUBLE BIRDS.

$100   10 per cent entrance   Purse to fill   Plunge Traps   Five Double Birds   First Prize $50
Second Prize, $30   Third Prize, $20

SWEEPSTAKES, $100.   10 per cent. entrance.

Open to all comers in New England   Wild Birds   Plunge Traps   10 Single Birds   One ounce
Shot   Eight entries to fill.   First Prize, $50   Second Prize, $30   Third Prize $20

☞ Shooting to commence each day at 10 o'clock.

For further information and circulars apply to JOSEPH TONKS, Gun Dealer, 45 Union St Boston

J. McIntire, Printer, 41 Federal Street, Boston

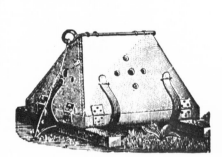 

Live pigeon shooting, following the English pattern, was a popular sport when the Golden Age began. The scene at top shows a typical English trap lay-out (Hornsey Wood), and the pigeon trap is an early English pattern.

The Bogardus glass-ball trap and some of the targets it threw. The clear glass and amber colored balls came first, followed by the corrugated ball, which prevented shot from glancing off, and the pitch or tar-type composition ball.

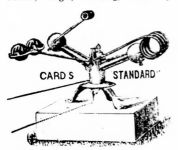
Though the Bogardus trap was the most widely accepted, it was by no means without rivals. Above are shown some of the better known ones.

BOGARDUS'S PATENT GLASS-BALL TRAP.

Capt. Adam H. Bogardus, and the trap he invented as it looked in use.

The California Sensation!!

DR. W. F. CARVER,
OF CALIFORNIA,
THE CHAMPION RIFLE SHOT OF THE WORLD

Dr. W. F. Carver could (and did) claim to be the finest shot of his era with any weapon. Star of Buffalo Bill's first Wild West Shows, he barnstormed the country with Bogardus to popularize clay pigeons, and in a series of 25 exhibition matches won 19. However, their "Match of the Century" for a $10,000 stake never came off.

FIRST INTERNATIONAL CLAY PIGEON TOURNAMENT,

UNDER THE AUSPICES OF THE

LIGOWSKY CLAY PIGEON COMPANY,

A Five Days' Programme, to be Held at

Chicago, Illinois, May, 1884.

Principal Contest: International Championship Match;

CONDITIONS.

Club team shooting (5 to a team); third notch of trap, 10-bore and 12-bore guns allowed; ten single birds, 18 yards rise; 5 double birds, 15 yards rise; Ranelagh Club Rules to govern, (excepting: use of single barrel only allowed), and such changes as managers may determine to meet wishes of shooters. Five traps screened, 3 yards apart. Special prize donated by the Ligowsky Clay Pigeon Company:—**To the winning team, $750; to the best individual score, $250 Diamond Badge.** Entrance fees, $25 per team. Entrance fees and gate money, less cost of birds, grounds and advertising, to be distributed as Second, Third, Fourth and Fifth Team Prizes—40, 30, 20 and 10 per cent. Should less than fifty duly organized clubs enter this match, then a club can enter as many teams of five as it may see fit.

A series of "Sweepstakes" will be interspersed with and follow the preceeding.

Headquarters in Chicago at the Palmer House.

Arrangements will be made for reduced railroad rates and hotel charges.

Clubs should enter at once, by remitting $1.00 to the undersigned. Balance of entrance money payable on the grounds at Chicago, on first day of shoot, to the General Manager and Representative of the Ligowsky Clay Pigeon Company.

Copies of the rules can be obtained by applying to the undersigned, to whom all communications on the subject should be addressed.

Further detailed list of matches, prizes, donors, etc., will be subsequently announced, together with exact date, grounds, etc. (Signed)

THE LIGOWSKY CLAY PIGEON CO.

20 7 P. O. Box 1292. Office, No. 68 W. Third St., Cincinnati, Ohio.

George Ligowsky ushered in the modern era of trap shooting by devising the first truly practical "clay" pigeon, and a trap to throw it. His first tournament nonetheless proved something of a bust. Ligowsky's products, too, had many imitators, as shown on the opposite page.

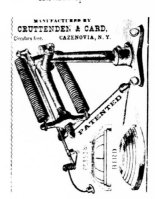

EXPERT TRAP

Old Reliable Blue Rock Pigeon.

$7.00 PER 1,000.

Paul North, shown operating the Magautrap above, was the guiding genius of the Chamberlin Cartridge and Target Co. in the late 1800's. The "Expert" and "Blue Rock" brands he popularized are still sold by Remington.

Rolla O. "Pop" Heikes, a Dayton, Ohio professional, was a famous live-bird shooter of the 1800's who successfully made the transition to clay targets, winning the first Grand American Handicap at targets with a score of 91 x 100 from 22 yards in 1900.

CHARLES SCHOENHEIDER, JR.

A typical market hunter of the Golden Age—the famous Peoria, Illinois duck hunter and decoy maker, Charles Schoenheider.

The Original Lefaucheux Breech-loader : 1836.

The advent of the breechloader was accompanied by considerable experimentation with lock-up systems (note the Fox, Lefaucheux and Hyde & Shattuck examples above) before the top lever came into general use.

Most shooters of the Golden Age had started with muzzle loaders, and were accustomed to purchasing bulk components. At first they were slow to adopt smokeless powders.

TO SPORTSMEN.

*Compared with any other, will
be found Cleaner, Heavier,
and more Uniform.*

Founded July 4, 1808.

Thos. W. Sparks,
Shot & Bar Lead
MANUFACTURER.

Office 121 Walnut Street, Philadelphia.

*Shot manufacturers, too, vied eagerly in the advertising pages for the favor
of sportsmen.*

Powder and Shot Measures.

Combined Powder and Shot Measures.

Hand-loading equipment available in the 1880's consisted mainly of single-stage tools, the "Ideal" brand shown at left being among the most popular.

More elaborate equipment included the Rapid Loader and Crimper, which claimed a rate of 100 shells in 7 minutes, and the Belcher, which tacitly suggested that it was safe for cigar smokers.

Manufactured shot shells attained virtually their present form, as well as their modern form of packaging, well before 1900.

Head-stamps from the author's collection of old shot shells. The C.C.&T. Co. imprint is Chamberlin's. Note the variety of primer sizes.

Three-Barrelled Breech-Loading Guns,
TWO SHOT AND ONE RIFLE.

A new feature in the Sporting Line. Forms a light and compact gun from eight to ten pounds giving to sportsmen the very thing so often wanted in all kinds of shooting.

PRICE:—Three barrel, $75 to $150. Double barrel shot guns, Damascus barrel, $50 to $100. Twist barrel, $35.

SEND FOR NEW CIRCULAR.

W. H. BAKER & CO., Syracuse, New York.

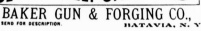

The BAKER IS ABSOLUTELY SAFE.

BAKER GUN & FORGING CO.,
SEND FOR DESCRIPTION.   BATAVIA, N. Y.

C. G. Bonehill's Special Guns.

THE COLT CLUB GUN.

It should be remembered that while we are the chief distributors of the regular Guns, we are SOLE AGENTS in New York for the COLT CLUB GUNS. The marked performance of these guns in pigeon and glass ball trap shooting is so well known no word of commendation is necessary. Every genuine Colt Club Gun has the heel plate with the words "The Club Gun" around a circle, within which appears a rampant colt beautifully embossed.

We also have a small remnant of Hollis and Webley breech loaders, mostly heavy ducking guns, at about half price.   Address

H. & D. FOLSOM, 15 Murray St., New York
P. O. Box 1,614

Guns and makers of the Golden Age. On this and the following six pages is shown a sampling of gun advertisements by some of the leading makers of the era, illustrating the various forms of hammer and hammerless double-barrel breechloader that were most characteristic of the period. (Further information about these makers appears in Appendix A.)

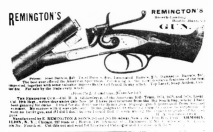

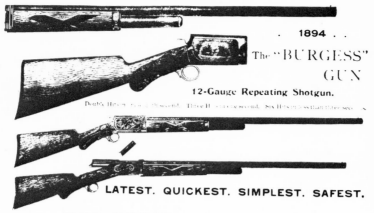

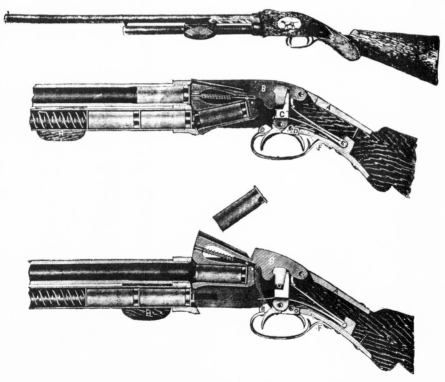

The eventual demise of the double-barrel shotgun was foreshadowed by the Burgess action, above, with its sliding pistol-grip, and the Spencer, below, which was actuated by a sliding forearm like modern pump guns.

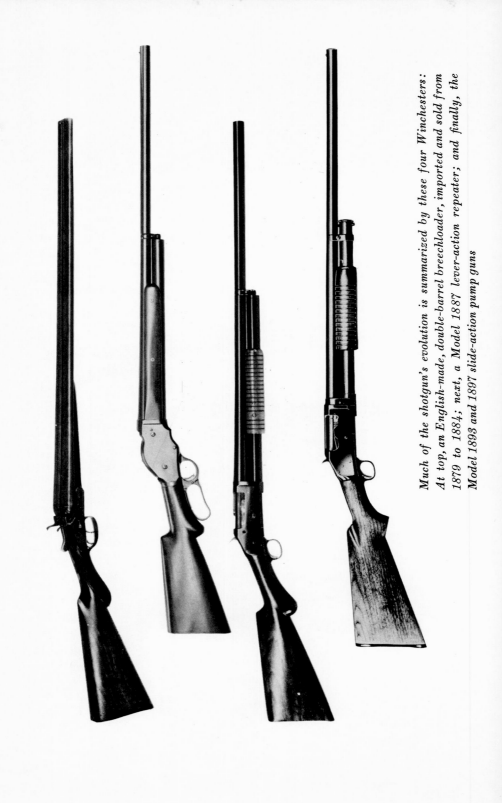

Much of the shotgun's evolution is summarized by these four Winchesters: At top, an English-made, double-barrel breechloader, imported and sold from 1879 to 1884; next, a Model 1887 lever-action repeater; and finally, the Model 1893 and 1897 slide-action pump guns

not brittle enough to break with certainty. Formulas of pitch, resin, and even celluloid were tried and failed.

Then the Composition Target Ball Co., of Lockport, New York, found a recipe that assured good breakage when hit and was the same weight as glass. These were sold in 1884 at $3 per barrel and highly advertised in the sporting papers of the time.

Even so, the old-time pigeon shooter was something less than excited about shooting glass balls. They were much too easy a target after pigeons, and the fact that they broke, and that-was-that, left the shooter with the feeling that something was lacking. To liven things a bit, balls were filled with dust, flour, and other markers to leave a puff of "smoke" when hit. The most famous and successful of these were perhaps Ira Paine's feather-filled balls, and Powell's Patent Puff Balls, as made by Henry Sears.

Powell's ball could be reused even when hit, and its claim to fame was no broken glass or fragments of clay on the ground. They could even be used on private lawns. They used no explosive compounds to make them dangerous in handling and transportation because they were made of paper and filled with dust. One ball was good for ten hits, and they were put up 100 in a box at $6.50. It cost you another $.25 to buy the puff ball perforator. This was simply a six-pronged affair with which you punched holes around the ball to allow the dust to escape when the ball was hit.

Ira Paine's feather-filled balls were made by Bohemian Glass Works, and simply contained domestic chicken and guinea hen feathers that floated gently to earth as the ball was broken. This supposedly gave the shooter a feeling of having downed a feathered bird. But the most success accorded them was by Mr. Paine himself, who used them in a series of theatrical appearances. It is possible the cost of $18 per thousand in 1878 was also a deterrent to their popularity.

Also in '78 Fowler & Folsom Co., of New York, sold Col. Fletcher's Bell-Metal Ball. These were said to be of a tempered brass, giving a loud ring when hit. But they were much heavier than glass balls and consequently flew more slowly and to less distance. Henry Squires, of New York, sold Marshall's glass balls for $5 per thousand in 1877. These were said to have been made by the Front Street Glass & Bottle Works, of Brooklyn.

1878 was the year of the great yellow fever epidemic. New Orleans and Memphis were particularly hard struck with over 9,000 persons dying in those two cities alone. It was also the year Doc Carver brought his Wild West Show to New York and gave an exhibition of breaking glass balls from the back of a running horse. At the end of each performance he pleaded for money to help relieve the suffering of fever victims, and was instrumental in getting gun clubs to hold special shoots with proceeds going to yellow fever relief. Many clubs in the South used a special yellow glass ball, packed 300 to the barrel, on which was stenciled, "Beat the yellow scourge." But I can find no mention of what firm actually manufactured this target.

In 1880 Woeber & Varwig, Cincinnati, Ohio, offered a ball called "Standard Clay Percussion Target Ball." It was said that when penetrated by a single pellet it would explode in a flash accompanied by a dense cloud of smoke, and offer undisputable proof of having been hit. D. H. Eaton in his book describes it as follows:

> The shot cannot glance from the surface of the ball. A heavy charge such as is necessary to break a glass ball is not needed. The ball can be burst at 100 yards, where a glass ball only shows marks of the shot. The balls are of uniform weight and furnished in any desired color. The objection to the debris of glass is avoided in this ball as the material is light pottery clay and burnt so it will not resist the action of the weather. They are stronger than glass and do not break easily when striking the ground.

The balls were said to be perfectly harmless and could be exploded in the hand without danger. They were priced at $15 per thousand.

While Mr. Eaton's book spells it Woeber, and Amos Woeber, of Cincinnati, did receive a patent on a target trap in 1885, there is a possibility the true name was Webber & Varwig. Webber, also of Cincinnati, is known to have invented an explosive ball, and H. Varwig was a Cincinnati capitalist who interested himself in it as he did later with Mr. Franzmann and his explosive "paper pigeon."

Varwig also advanced the money to Al Bandel, famous Cincinnati shooter and shoot promoter, for an experimental target called the Red Devil. This was a clear glass ball stuffed with a compressed, red crepe paper, supposed to spring out and expand into streamers as the ball was broken. While seemingly one of many for Mr. Varwig, it was the first of Bandel's follies on inanimate targets.

Eaton also lists the Smoke Target Ball Co., of Titusville, Pennsylvania, with the date 1884 and little other mention. However, reports of the time state that these balls were so affected by damp weather as to be useless, and were soon off the market. Other makes of balls noted editorially or in advertisements were the Mole, Holden, and Kimber Composition. There were undoubtedly many more of which I have been unable to find record.

The early ball traps were hidden behind a screen so that the shooter could not see what angle it was set. The puller could change the angle of the trap by cords attached to a crosspiece, the same as tiller ropes on a boat. Even so, glass ball shooting was not particularly demanding of great skill. This was quickly noted by famous shooters of the day, who rather than shoot twenty-five or 100-bird matches preferred long runs, endurance contests, or to shoot against time. Bogardus, Paine, and Carver all shot in this manner, and all could be expected to break 1,000 balls within an hour and a half shooting time. Bogardus once shot at 5,000 balls in 500 minutes, missing only 156 for a total of 4,844 broken.

It was perhaps because of the ease with which a shooter of average ability could run a good score that glass balls became so popular. Those who could count on a score only in the low fifties or sixties per 100 live birds could easily become an eighty or even ninety per cent shooter on glass. But those of great shotgunning skill soon tired of the glass ball and the search began anew for more novel and harder inanimate targets. Some of these took odd forms.

E. E. Thresher, of Akron, Ohio, invented the steel passenger pigeon — three metal pigeon silhouettes strung on a cable and flushed in rapid succession by a pulley arrangement. Along the same lines was an English invention, the Jones Snipe Throwing Trap — a catapult throwing a large metal bird that had a twisting flight of fifty to sixty yards and gave a puff of blue powder when hit. An inflated rubber bladder could also be attached.

In 1884 the G. F. Kolb Co., of Philadelphia, proudly offered Belcher's Patent Paper Bird, a stiff paper cutout attached to a wire ball which could be thrown from any glass ball trap. The idea being the bird could be used again after picking it up and marking the shot perforations. And the usual claim to set it apart from the glass ball, "no broken glass or clay to injure the grounds." It was sold fifty paper birds and one ball for $1. It was not popular and Mr. Belcher's fortune, if any, was made on his automatic shotshell reloading machine rather than his targets.

Globe Flights was advertised as the "Perfect Target" in 1884. It was sold by the Globe Shot Co., of St. Louis, and was a pasteboard disk five and a half inches in diameter with center cut out to accommodate a rubber balloon. The selling price was $20 per thousand with a refund of $2.50 per thousand for the pasteboard disks if received in good condition.

The gyro pigeon enjoys a measure of success in England, even today where it is known as the ZZ target. We had it here in 1872 under the name of the Bussey Patent Gyro Pigeon. In that year it was fairly popular and gyro shooting was considered a form apart from the glass ball — often a separate shoot being held after the regular live bird or glass ball program. The "trap" was a box containing a coil spring with a spindle in its center. The spindle rapidly revolved when the spring uncoiled and the bird itself resembled the blade of a propeller. When rapidly revolved and set free from the trap it rose straight into the air rather slowly but to great distance. The trap was sold complete with winding key, 100 birds, an extra spring for $25. Mr. Eaton remarks that, "The invention had a ready sale in England, France, Belgium, and India, and to some extent in America."

Many substitutes for live birds were tried and discarded in the 70s and early 80s, but generally, the glass ball was king. Its reign was to be a short one, however, for in the end the innumerable varieties of live-bird substitutes were to prove merely targets of transition. Perhaps its death knell sounded at what might be called the predecessor of the Grand American Handicap. This was the Chicago 1884 "First National Inanimate Target Tourney" described in the next chapter. Only a handful of shooters were there — but the targets were Ligowsky's new clay pigeons, not glass balls.

[CHAPTER FIVE]

Clay Birds

THE YEAR 1880 was an inventive one. George Eastman delighted the amateur photographer with roll film. Edison, at long last, perfected his incandescent light bulb. Woolworth started his ten cent stores at Lancaster, Pennsylvania. The Kampfe Brothers devised the safety razor, which was quickly denounced by the barbering trade.

As far as the shotgunner was concerned, 1880 was notable for the flying clay pigeon. In that year the New York State Game Association encamped at Coney Island and presented the largest attended live bird shoot of its time. At the end of the regular program was the first public exhibition of a new inanimate target described in the shoot program as follows:

> The last contest is a shoot at flying clay pigeons. The pigeon consists of a clay disk and on being thrown from the trap sails a long distance with considerable speed. Only a small surface is presented to the shooter and it requires more quickness and skill than shooting at glass balls. They are to be shot ten birds at eighteen and fifteen yards rise.

Reports at the time tell of it being a lively and suitable substitute that was sorely needed as a target replacement for the live
bird. The fact that not every live bird shooter accepted it as such
was only natural, but the glass ball era had accomplished about all
that could be expected and the many substitutions such as metal
birds running along a wire and other ingenious devices had failed to
interest or amuse the dedicated live bird shot. Now the "flying clay
disk" had proven to be a target of merit and it was the start of a
new era in shotgun shooting.

Many individuals laid claim to have invented the first clay pigeon,
but substantiation is largely lacking except in the case of George
Ligowsky of Cincinnati, Ohio. Ligowsky, who is said to have gotten
his idea from watching boys skipping clamshells on the water, tried
some forty different designs of disks before finally settling on the
domed saucer shape which he patented in 1880.

Ligowsky's first clay pigeons were made, appropriately enough,
of clay. They were baked in cast-iron molds, and heated in a long,
narrow furnace. It was a red clay, ground and mixed with water to a
gravy-like consistency. Each mold was filled by syphon hose from a
barrel of the mixture, and then placed to bake. After baking, the
birds were then removed and placed in a brick kiln for a second firing.

It was an extremely hard target giving off a bell-like sound when
hit, and could sometimes be knocked completely off its flight by shot,
without breaking. Soft shot was much in use, but even so, richocheting
shot from the target was a shooter hazard.

Variance in temperature of the kilns made little difference in
bricks, but often overburned the clay pigeon making it hard as rock.
Targets were picked up with as many as six pellet holes and having
been called lost birds because of no visible breakage during flight.

These first targets were made with a small tongue of pasteboard
glued to the edge of the bird and it was this that was held by the
trap arm. It was also this tongue that gave problems either from
inferior cardboard lips or bad glue, or both. It was not waterproof,
so clay pigeon shooting was a fair weather sport. When the target
was damp it was simply unmanageable. In later Ligowsky and Fisher
patents this tongue was made of clay and integral with the bird itself.

But there was still much rumbling that the bird was hard to break
even when hit squarely. So much so that a Mr. Hills, of the Cincinnati

Gun Club, made the following experiment in 1881 and recorded it in *The American Field,*

> It has been claimed that clay pigeons are hard to break. The fact is that they are more easily broken than glass balls and I have made experiments to prove this to be true. Anyone can do so themselves by placing a clay pigeon and a glass ball side by side and shooting at sixty-five yards. You will find out of ten shots you will break nine clay pigeons and only one glass ball.

However, this experiment may be slightly colored. Although it did not state so in the report, Mr. Hills was in the employ of the Ligowsky Clay Pigeon Co. The consensus of the shooters of that day was that the clay pigeon was "damn near impossible to break."

But the idea was there, and it looked good. Now it only remained to develop a target that could be easily broken by the shot charge, but not so fragile as to be broken by the trap or in transportation. So in the next five years a great many formulas were developed with birds being made from tar, plaster of paris, different types of pottery clay, and river bottom silt.

Al Bandel, of Kentucky, who was a well-known shoot promoter, as well as shooter, developed a target called the "lark," made almost exclusively of tar and which worked well in cold weather, but any sort of warmth made it soft and likely to be misshapen by the throw of the trap.

Fred Kimble, of Peoria, is claimed to have introduced the first composition target about 1884 which he called the "Peoria Blackbird." This was made of river silt and plaster of paris in almost the same proportions as the Kimber composition ball made in 1881. Since Kimber and Kimble were known to have been friends, it may be assumed Kimble was given the formula by Mr. Kimber.

By 1882 we find that birds were not now hard to break and had run to the extreme opposite end of the coin. Clay targets were sold by the barrel, and as one shoot report cited, "We had a barrel sent by express and tried to break as many as the express company did. But they beat us and should be given the medal."

However, the clay pigeon, in spite of its faults, was so superior to other forms of inanimate targets that the shooter was willing to suffer inconvenience. The Ligowsky trap differed little in principle from those of today. But it was claimed "complicated and none but an expert can handle." This was probably true when compared to the catapult-type ball trap.

The Ligowsky company recommended their trap be set on a framework of inch plank, about four feet long and two feet wide, this framework being secured to the earth by driving two wide wooden pins through the boards on each side. They also admonished keeping the clamp which grasped the tongue of the pigeon clean and dry. The tongue was placed in a clamp on the left side of the trap arm, which was pulled back until caught by the pawl. There were two of these pawls, or checks, and the velocity of the bird could be increased by engaging the pawl farthest back.

Now that the clay pigeon and its trap had a firmly established market, other firms began manufacture of the same type of bird and trap with minor alterations in design, thus hoping to avoid infringement of the Ligowsky patents. But an attorney, J. E. Bloom, had become general manager of the Ligowsky firm and smiled not at the blatant efforts of other to "steal" his company's market.

We now entered several years of what was to become known as the clay pigeon controversy. A patent was granted Ligowsky on September 7, 1880. There were two claims — one for the tongue and one for the shape of the target. Two years eight months later, Nicholas Fischer was granted a patent almost identical. Fischer assigned his patent to the American Claybird Company, and as soon as it was recorded, he filed suit against Ligowsky through his attorneys, Hosea and Merrill. Ligowsky then filed a counter suit. Claims and counterclaims were to keep both companies busy in court for over two years.

But a decree was entered with the finding that Ligowsky was first to make the device, and declared Fischer's patent void, and the plaintiff to pay court costs. Then Ligowsky filed suit against the American Claybird Company claiming their Marqua trap was an infringement of Ligowsky's trap patents. Ligowsky also defended three other parties — Tiepel, Spangler, and Kirkwood — against Marqua, claiming they had all preceded him in the invention. But these were decided in favor of Mr. Marqua and American Claybird, leading Mr. Bloom to state the three most uncertain things in the world were, "Where lightning would strike, whether a woman would say yes or no, and what the verdict of a jury would be." Over forty traps were patented between Ligowsky's original and 1900. Over seventy different brands were offered on the market, whether patented or not. And some of them were found definitely superior to Ligowsky's.

J. E. Bloom resigned from the Ligowsky firm he had brought through such stormy seas, and resumed his law practice in New York in 1887. Without his business acumen, inventive mind, and ability to get things done, the Ligowsky firm went into a steep decline from which it never recovered. But there were still hundreds of other makers hoping their target design and formula would be the shooters' choice.

The English referred to the new target as a "sphere." We called them inanimate targets, muds, clay pigeons, asphalts, flying discs, river bottoms, baked birds, traps, and blackbirds. White Flyer's ads called your attention to their "New Soil Disks."

By 1887 the clay pigeon was presented in different and distinctive appearance from many makers. Some could only be thrown from traps made for a particular brand of bird, some had one or two "ears," and some were without tongues.

Ligowsky was now pushing the Mueller Trap #7 which threw their new and improved target with a clay tongue and inturned edge. The company claimed this bottom edge survived shipping, trapping, and falling to the ground much better, producing "the surest breaker when hit and surest non-breaker when not hit." They were sold to clubs for three-quarters of a cent each, and Ligowsky offered to exchange their new trap for other makes without charge.

The American Shot & Lead Co., of Chicago, offered the American Target, and there was another "American" made by the American Mfg. Co., of Baltimore, which also offered a pneumatic trap. The American Claybird Co., of Cincinnati, was offering birds in their #1 New Model, and #2 Old Model. Their advertising stated, "Our New Birds for easier shooting, our Old Birds for clubs preferring hard shooting," the main difference being the New Bird had a higher dome.

The Niagara Flying Target Co. said their "Niagara Falls Blackbird" would sail against the wind without raising and was the only target to do so. They were priced at $10 a thousand, and used the motto, "Not much to look at but a rare un to go." It was claimed they could be thrown from any trap, but the clay tongue of the bird was thinner and set higher than many traps would take. Their own trap sold for $5.

The New Lockport Bat by the Lockport Target Co., of Lockport, New York, contained a wooden tongue and only flew successfully from the Bat Trap or Ligowsky. Their motto was, "The best and cheapest target on earth."

Cruttenden & Card, Cazenovia, New York, offered the King Bird without tongue which was almost as popular as the Peoria Blackbird. That target was made by Stock and Kimble who now called themselves the Peoria Target Co., for clay pigeons, and the Blackbird Trap Co., for traps. This was the original "Blackbird" and certainly the most popular clay pigeon in use at the end of the 80's. It was a molded target of coal tar and gypsum, said later to be changed to tar and river silt. The factory was in Averyville, now the north end of Peoria.

The Parkersburg Target Co., of Parkersburg, Iowa, made a metal target of heavy tin that could be thrown from Blackbird, Macomber, and Blue Rock traps. When hit, it was supposed to drop down a large wire ring and settle quickly to the ground. While the company guaranteed it to do so when struck by only two pellets of #8 shot, shoot reports state it did not perform as advertised. There was also a Parkersburg Target Co., of Evanston, Illinois, which made both a claybird and trap arm to fit the Peoria Blackbird trap. I cannot substantiate whether or not the above companies were one and the same.

The Macomber Target Co., of St. Paul, offered a metal target claimed good for 100 hits. Its advertising claimed, "Does not break, but drops instantly when hit fairly. No disputes about broken birds." Targets cost $7.50 per box of fifty, and traps were listed for $5 each.

The Champion Tin Target Co., at Canal and Randolph Streets, Chicago, offered a bird of that construction, which was said to be about the worst target ever invented. W. T. Best was the inventor. He claimed any pellet striking the target would release a flange to hang down and retard the flight like that of a wing-tipped bird. But in practice the flange was so stiff a bird could be perforated with shot without its release, or else so sensitively set that the jar of the trap would release it.

The Star Flyer Target was made in Ft. Wayne, Indiana and seems to have been made only during 1887. The Lafayette Target Co., of Lafayette, Indiana, made a feather-filled target in two models — with and without tongue. Their ads said, "The coming bird — nearest approach to the live bird ever made." It was $14 per thousand.

The Markle Lead Works, of St. Louis, offered the Universal Target. It was constructed with very thin walls for easy breaking, but reinforced rims to increase pick-ups. Since there were more fifty than ninety per cent shooters in the clubs of that day, the re-use of grounded targets was considered quite a savings to the club. But the Universal's walls were too thin and trap breakage was large. It did not become popular and had a shortterm sale at $3.50 per thousand.

In the 90's the White Flyer target, then as now, was very popular and made by the Western Trap & Target Co., of St. Louis.

Keystone Target Co., of New York and Chicago, made traps and a clay pigeon called the Standard, their claim to fame being that ten traps had thrown 30,000 birds without breaking over a half-dozen. It was a popular target.

The United States Pigeon Co., of Findlay, Ohio, made the U.S. Pigeon under the directorship of Fred Damm who had left Cleveland Target Co. in 1892. They were on the market only a short time.

H. Varwig, of Cincinnati, took another financial flyer with Charles Franzmann who invented the explosive Blue Rock Paper Pigeon. It was made entirely of pasteboard covered with fulminate and that in turn covered with a thick coating of white sand to give the bird the required weight. When struck by shot, it was intended that the fulminate would explode leaving a volume of smoke. The inventor claimed they were not dangerous to handle, and were as cheap as clay birds. They were shipped in lots of 500 to the barrel, and thrown from the Ligowsky trap. There is only one known tournament in which they were used, and were said not to be satisfactory. But they were withdrawn from the market because Ligowsky had started suit claiming an infringement regarding the shape of the tongue used.

Other target brands of the 90's and early 1900's were "Dickey Bird" made in Boston by arrangement with the W. S. Dickey Clay Mfg. Co., of Kansas City, Missouri, who also made the target and supplied it to the Western states; a "Star" target, made in Covington, Kentucky; the "Tribune," of Erie, Pennsylvania; another two "Blackbirds," one made by Garlick Co., Cincinnati, and one in Knoxville, Tennessee.

But as the new century approached, two brands appeared to have the lead — the "White Flyer" and the "Blue Rock." The Blue Rock was a product of the closely intertwined Chamberlin Cartridge & Target Co. and the Cleveland Target Co. Eaton's book implies the

Blue Rock was made by the Atlantic Ammunition Co., but they were only the Eastern distributor.

As the nineteenth century drew to a close, the clay pigeon achieved a standard in quality and shape differing little from the target in use today. But great improvements were being made in traps. Some of these were automatic, magazine traps complete with electric release.

The clay pigeon was firmly established as *the* inanimate target, rapidly growing in popularity and replacing live birds. Although the pigeon match was still being held, using domestic birds, it was now called "pigeon shooting" and had relinquished its long-held name of "trapshooting" to the clay pigeon.

The first national trapshooting tournament for clay pigeons is generally credited to a meeting at New Orleans, La., February 11–16, 1885, and held under the auspices of the National Gun Association.

According to my findings, however, it was ante-dated by the First National Inanimate Target Tourney, held in Chicago May, 1884 by the Ligowsky Clay Pigeon Co. It was to be a team shoot, five to a team, with ten single birds eighteen yards rise, and five double birds fifteen yards rise, five traps screened three yards apart. Added money of $750 to the winning team and a $250 diamond badge to the best individual scorer.

The shoot headquarters were at the Palmer House Hotel, and special arrangements were made for reduced railroad fares and hotel charges. But it turned out to be a bust — only a handful of shooters showed up. Thus I'm willing to concede that the New Orleans shoot was at least the first *successful* national tournament. There the number of competitors was light, but the names were the greatest in the business at that time. They included Capt. A. H. Bogardus, Dr. W. F. Carver, Harvey McMurchy, Al Bandle, Ben Teipel, T. Gastright, J. A. R. Elliott, Andy Meaders, O. R. Dickey, Ed Voris, F. L. Chamberlain,[1] J. R. Stice, Frank Parmelee, W. S. Perry, H. W. Eager, C. M. Stark, Capt. Stubbs, Kirkwood, and Riley. Of these nineteen names, at least half stood to benefit in other than prize money. They were "pros" in more ways than one — either as manufacturers or representatives of manufacturers for guns, shells, or target equipment.

---

1 Probably Frank Chamberlin.

The matches were shot over five traps, as was the custom of the day, the traps being reloaded after each shot, and only one man on the firing line at a time. The firing order was determined by lot. And this is the way early claybirding was done, because in the beginning it followed as nearly as possible the customs and rules of live pigeon shooting.

When the clay pigeon first replaced the glass ball, its beginning purpose was to offer practice more closely simulating live bird shooting. However, with the scarcity of birds, the pigeon match was held less frequently and the clay pigeon assumed greater popularity. Within a two-year span we find it becoming a sport of itself. And since numerous shoots were being held, it was only natural that many were called championships.

It was soon noted that a governing body other than those with a vested interest (such as the gun and target makers) was needed to set uniform rules and see to their enforcement. Several attempts were made to do just this. But the associations were not accredited in the eyes of the shooter or most clubs. Their rulings carried little weight.

The first of record was the Inanimate Bird Shooting Association (also the name of the first English clay pigeon association). The first of influence was the American Shooting Assn., organized February 11, 1889. Its president was Charles W. Dimick, and among its directors were L. C. Smith and Chas. Tatham. Its advisory board, among others, included W. Fred Quimby, Harvey McMurchy, Al Bandle, R. B. Organ, and A. W. DuBray. With such illustrious and influential names, here was an association to command respect, even though they too were connected with industry.

But, as has been known to happen within trapshooting, then and since, there were dissenters, and many of these carried equally influential names. In fact, some of the originators of the ASA changed camps. Three years later we find the ASA voice had been replaced completely by the Interstate Manufacturers & Dealers Assn. Its original purpose was to promote the sport, whereby more shells and targets would be used to the benefit of the manufacturers. But it also laid the groundwork for trapshooting as we know it today.

By 1895 the name was changed to "The Interstate Association" under the capable managership of Elmer Shaner. He had formerly been with the Pennsylvania State Sportsmen's Association for Trap, which had used Shaner's original ideas for registered shooting — an excellent idea that did not meet national acceptance until some time later.

The first mention I can find of a classification system is in the form of a letter to *Forest & Stream* in 1887. A writer from Indianapolis, signing himself "Richmond," suggested that all trapshooters be classified fifty, sixty, seventy, eighty, and ninety per cent, and that the clubs keep records for six months or a year. The writer believed clubs could then "have shoots that everybody will attend." The English were first to use yardage handicap, but gave it up as dangerous when "shooting down the line."

But in the early 90's there was still no real standard of either classification or handicap, and the Sunday shooter stood alongside the professional trying for the same championship. It wasn't until 1898 that the rules called for the professional to stop shooting for money and the amateur at last had a chance to make expenses.

The rules of both live bird and clay pigeon shooting were in a state of change during the last decade of the nineteenth century. One of great controversy was whether the gun be allowed to be mounted to the shoulder before calling for the target. It was first permitted in 1891, much to the disgust and complaint of the old-time shooter whose style had always been to call for his bird with gun down.

Clay target "championships" were now being held everywhere for everything. It became commonplace for target or ammunition companies to conduct clay target shoots, and one of the earliest to do so was the Chamberlin Cartridge and Target Co. of Cleveland, producers of the Blue Rock target and the "Expert" trap later sold to Remington. Chamberlin's "First Annual Tournament" was held in 1894, but it was preceded by a number of tournaments which were not termed "annual." An officer of Chamberlin and its parent, the Cleveland Target Co., was Paul North, who developed the North system of handicapping and prize money distribution, and invented the electric trap release, patented in 1891.

Himself a high-average shooter, North and the company he managed exerted a considerable influence on the development of trap shooting. Around 1897 Chamberlin marketed the Magautrap, built on a bicycle-like frame and run by pedals, and in November of 1898 they rigged it to operate electrically, and thus created the first fully automatic trap. A success from the beginning, the Magautrap eventually changed the whole game of trapshooting from one in which five traps were used to the present single trap.

Another early nationally recognized trophy shoot on inanimate targets was that sponsored by the powder manufacturers, E.C., which commenced in 1896. As the century closed, many tournaments formerly using live birds had come over to the clay pigeon, and it was not uncommon for a championship shoot to have over a hundred entries. The possibility of using inexpensive targets and a single trap meant that every town and village could afford a gun club, and many weren't long in starting one. As the new century arrived, trapshooting was at a new height of popularity.

CHAPTER SIX

Crack Shots

A FAVORITE pastime of the sporting *aficionado* has always been comparing then and now, matching up the past and present greats of various sporting activities in imaginary contests.

This game can be played by those interested in the world of tournament trapshooting, too. Where would the money go today if a five-man squad composed of Rolla Heikes, Fred Gilbert, J. A. R. Elliott, W. R. Crosby, and C. W. Budd, were pitted against the best men we can field today? And how many years will this game continue, with Carver and Bogardus representing the past, against the greatest champions of the future?

Of course, the best part of the game is that there is no definitive result. Any champion is only the best of his own time, and that is the best anyone can be. The equipment and rules change, even if man does not, and there is no fair comparison to be made.

But, if America were to name but one all-time, all-around champion of the shotgun, a chief candidate would be Adam H. Bogardus. He was born in Albany, N.Y. but moved to central Illinois as a young boy. In 1850 it was a "western" state with prairies and marshlands filled with game. His first shooting was done at ruffed grouse and woodcock in the East. No one taught him — he had a natural gift. On settling near the Sangamon River, he quickly made a name for himself, as Bogardus was a large, powerful man of great strength and endurance — a great asset for the type of outdoor life he chose to lead.

His earlier days of market hunting are well described in his book, *Field, Cover & Trapshooting*, published in 1874. At that time shooting was a trade and an art, as much so as boat building or surgery. And Bogardus was not only a skilled shooter, but a showman and promoter as well. He was intelligent, perceptive, possessed of a highly inventive mind and imagination. Ambiguous and egotistical, he could not tolerate being second — a trait which led many to claim he would win fairly if he could, if not, by any means possible.

He undoubtedly would have been a champion at anything he chose. The facts show he was a great shot in a time of great shooters. Many of his records still stand, although admittedly because they would seem pointless today. Who would be interested in shooting 5,000 glass balls in 500 minutes today, and what would he really accomplish? But Bogardus did on one hot Fourth of July at Lincoln, Ill., and he was widely acclaimed on the front pages of newspapers throughout the land. In 1879 our values were different; shooting was front page news. It was the day of the "shooting challenge" and *mano-a-mano* tournaments.

Moneyed people backed their champions and thousands of dollars in side bets rode on a single shot. Shooters such as Bogardus, Kleinman, and Carver were seldom at a loss to find someone willing to stack as much as 10,000 gold dollars on their ability to out-shoot all comers.

The *Chicago Tribune* and other metropolitan papers, as well as sporting magazines, especially *Spirit of the Times*, carried ads with challenges to and from champions and would-be's. They would read:

> I hereby challenge any man to face me at the traps on 100 live birds for $1,000 a side. Rules to be those of the New York Sportsmen's Club, and use any breechloader of 10 Ga. or less. The place and time to be decided upon by both parties, and a $250 forfeit payed on agreement, to be held by the business office of *Spirit of the Times*.

Many more challenges were made than contests actually shot. Advertisements were not expensive. If a man cared to, he could build the reputation of a champion without firing a gun. Some shooters of small ability would publish ads with this idea in mind and then find many reasons why they could not accept the challenge unless it was from someone they were positive they could beat.

The practice was so common, that the credence of a public challenge depended upon the signature. Those signed "A. H. Bogardus, 72 Madison Street, Chicago" were seldom answered without forfeit money in hand.

Modesty was not considered a virtue among the champion shooters — few of lasting fame were known for humility. Each loudly proclaimed he was *the* champion and that *no* man could out-shoot him. While some of this may have been professional showmanship, such as two fighters making faces from across the ring, it would appear that most animosity was truly felt.

An example was a September, 1883 challenge from Doc Carver to Capt. Stubbs to meet him. Carver wrote,

> In order to relieve the minds of one and all who think they possess more ability than myself as a shooter, I make the following proposition to the world. I will bet 5 to 1 to any amount that no man can beat me. I will wager from $1,000 to $5,000 and let my opponent select any one of the matches he wishes. If Mr. Harry Hill will back Capt. Stubbs against me for $5,000 a side, I will give him $500 for a present.

The matches suggested were 100 live pigeons thirty yards rise, or 100 clay pigeons and 100 glass balls at thirty yards rise, or shooting from the back of a running horse at twenty-one yards rise. The challenge was signed "Dr. W. F. Carver, Champion Pigeon Shot of the World."

While Bogardus was not mentioned, it seemed to rile him because he wrote to the *American Field* on October 20, 1883,

> I notice Dr. Carver signs himself "Pigeon Champion of the World." Now I will say to him that there cannot be two champions for one thing. I have been champion for 12 years and during that time was never defeated. Now I will say to Dr. Carver that I will put my cup up against his and shoot him for the championship of the world in three matches.

One of the matches Bogardus suggested was 100 pigeons with fifty birds to be double releases, and he specified they be shot in either Cincinnati, Chicago, or St. Louis, and that the matches be for $250, $500, or as much more as Carver wished to shoot for. Another $1,000 was to go to the winner of two out of three matches. Dr. Rowe, then editor of the *American Field*, was to hold the money and appoint a referee.

Bogardus went on to say,

> To show I mean business I enclose $250 as forfeit, and if the matches are not accepted by Dr. Carver they are open to any man in the world, one or all of them. I intended to withdraw from pigeon shooting when I was fifty years old, and that was the seventeenth day of September, but as there are two or three men who claim the title of champion, I will give them a chance to fairly win it from me as I do hold the championship of the world.

Bogardus received many replies from men wanting to shoot him for the title who had, unfortunately, neither money nor backers. The Carver-Stubbs match failed for the same reason when Stubbs' backer didn't appear and Carver refused to shoot.

Some of those turned down by Bogardus for lack of funds claimed he was afraid to meet them, and they would assume his title on default unless he did. Since $1,000 was a lot of money ninety years ago, there may have been some truth that, "Champions often protected their titles by dollars alone."

W. T. Mitchell was known as a great shooter, but not a man of means. He was turned down by Ira Paine, Carver, and Bogardus many times because he could not produce "hold" money in the amount for which they were willing to shoot.

Mitchell paid for an ad that appeared in the *Sportsmen's Journal* and that he hoped would create a public demand for a match. It read,

> It is useless to bandy words. Bogardus claims to be champion of the world and I hereby make a challenge to shoot a match for same at 100 pigeons for a side of $100. It is immaterial whether anyone thinks I can beat him except myself because I propose to put up my own money and leave it to the public to say whether Bogardus has the right to require me to put up $500 when the title is at stake. There is one other than myself who believes I can beat

him, and that is Bogardus himself, or he would not have such a dread of meeting with me. Now, Captain, if you are afraid to shoot, say so. If not, meet me like a man and a few hours before the traps will satisfy the public who is champion.

Mitchell's ad was in vain. There was no public clamor for the two men to meet, and evidently it excited Bogardus not the least. The two occasions on which Mitchell actually did meet Bogardus were rather disappointing, both to him and the public. The first time, after both Bogardus and Mitchell had killed fifty-nine out of sixty-one birds under Hurlingham rules, Bogardus withdrew, stating that there was no money on the line and the match had grown uninteresting to him.

Their next meeting in St. Louis was at 100 birds with a $500 side. Mitchell was shooting a 10-gauge against Bogardus' 12. Mitchell had gained a three-bird lead and Bogardus complained to the referee that he was not being out-shot, but out-gunned. He complained so loudly and vigorously that Mitchell consented to exchange guns and the match went on with the final score Bogardus eighty-six Mitchell eighty-four.

It was on his numerous tours of exhibition that Bogardus gained his greatest fame. For an eye-witness report we turn to a newspaper article headlined, "Bogardus' Big Score."

Capt. A. H. Bogardus, the champion wing-shot of the world, took upon himself last week one of those tremendous feats in the way of marksmanship for which he is now so famous. His match against time at 5,000 glass balls a year ago is familiar to all our readers, and his time then was far below the common. On several of the hundreds he broke at the rate of between eighteen and twenty a minute, loading at the time his own gun. The match of the eighth and ninth was one of accuracy rather than rapidity, and conditions required that he should break 6,000 glass balls, thrown at fifteen yards rise from a Bogardus trap. The wagers were $1,000 even that less than 6,200 would be fired at; $500 to $1,000 that not more than 6,100 would be used, and $100 to $1,000 that the break would be straight.

The Captain used his W. & C. Scott & Co. gun with two set of barrels of 10 and 12-gauge, using four and three and a half drams of Dittmar powder respectively, and one and a half ounces No. 8 Otis LeRoy & Co.'s tin-coated shot. The match opened at 11 o'clock on the morning of the 8th, and all the assistants were at their posts.

Dr. B. Talbot was puller, Miles Johnson, of New Jersey, and Elisha Garrison, of Syracuse, as referees, and T. C. Banks, scorer. An active lad kept the trap supplied with balls, and in answer to the "pull" of the champion, ball after ball rose in the air to be shattered instantly. Many expert shots from this and other states watched the perfect work. Now and then there was a trifling dispute about balls which fell seemingly whole. In one case a bit broken from the neck showed the work of the shot, and in another the load had passed completely through the sphere, without shattering it into the usual fragments. But from first to last of the match the referees were scrupulously careful in their rulings.

During the first half hundred shots the thumb-piece of the rigth hammer broke off, and though the Captain did for a time lift the hammer by pressing his thumb upon the broken and jagged fragment, the effort was very painful, and the majority of shots fired during the day were from the left barrel. The Captain shot easily, not hurrying himself and taking liberal rests, and from first to last every ball was declared broke, and but one misfire had occurred during the day.

The last 500 balls shot at on the first day were closely watched, for upon them hung a 1,000-ball match with Kleinman, of Chicago, in which Bogardus was to give his rival 200 broken balls, and at nine o'clock it was announced that 3,000 balls had been shattered without a miss. Cheers were given again and again. The Captain had then two long water blisters on his left thumb, burned by the hot barrels of his gun, and his right arm and shoulder were very, very stiff. Kleinman in his 400 shots missed only six balls, shooting, however, very much slower than the Captain, and using a Nichols & Lefevre gun with similar charges to those of Capt. Bogardus.

On the morning of Thursday, Capt. Bogardus was early at his work. The first ball of the fourth thousand was sprung on time, and the work for a while was a repetition of that done on the day before. When the Captain's stiff arm and bandaged hand had warmed to his work he made some very quick hundreds, firing for some time at the rate of from ten to twelve shots a minute. At 1:05 P.M., having broken 3,787 in all from the start, he took a recess for lunch. His next stop was at 3:05 at the 1,330th shot for the day, when he could barely distinguish the balls against the white canvas, and rested till 4:50, when the garden was lighted up.

His first miss was the 5,681st ball, a rapid dropper which he shot over. At this time he was evidently suffering considerably but he completed the hundred without another miss. He had rested from 8:04 to 8:20, and at 8:50 dropped again into a chair, where he sat until 9:15 during which time a new curtain was hung up. He was now getting into a very bad shooting form, but he kept on firing as best he could with the rapidly stiffening arm and fingers. Almost immediately after resuming his work came the next miss. In the next to the last hundred shots, the misses piled up rapidly. First, the 5,831st ball went down whole, then the 5,834th, then the 5,847th and 5,855th, 5,860th, 5,863rd, 5,866th, 5,867th, and 5,872nd; the markman's hands refusing to follow his eye. The last hundred was shot with unusual energy; No. 5,920 was the last miss.

It was about 9:30 when the Captain completed the breaking of the thirteen extra balls fired at to make up for those lost. Donning his ulster, the Captain sat down to see Kleinman finish his 400 shots. The Chicago champion began in good style, making but one miss in his first hundred, and two in each succeeding hundred, leaving the match a tie. The Captain was ready to go on and shoot off the tie, but Kleinman was too sore, and the tie will be shot off in a short time in Chicago, whither both men have gone.

To anyone but the Captain the test would have been a severe one, since but few others than he could have endured the pounding of so long a fusilade. In his style of holding and of hitting, the Captain was a model gunner.

Hits were central, and the balls were not merely winged or clipped, but fairly centered, and with the great charges which the champion delights to use, the glass spheres were blown to powder in almost every case. The balls were thrown at random, right and left, but the lightning speed with which they were covered and brought down made the old shooters present fairly alive with admiration.

With a record of 5,000 broken balls in 480 minutes already to his credit, as an exhibition of speed, the great wing shot of the world now had the unprecedented score of 6,000 in 6,013, or a run of 5,680 consecutive breaks; and yet he is not satisfied, but intends to carve his name yet higher on the scroll of shooting fame, and before the year is out we shall see what we shall see, and further the writer sayeth not.

Bogardus' records, matches, and exhibitions are much too numerous to list. Some he did himself in a lengthy letter mailed to the *American Field* in December, 1883 and I quote here in part,

> Twelve years ago I won the title of Champion Pigeon Shot of America. Since then, no one has wrested it from me. Upon going to England, I issued a challenge to the United Kingdom and faced adversaries in eighteen matches, all of which I won. I also won the medal as Champion Shot of the World, and in returning to England in 1878 captured a cup there for the same title.
>
> To give the public a better idea of my claim to champion, I

have challenged and beaten Mr. Paine, Kleinman, Tinker, and King. I have won thousands of dollars on challenges such as to kill 100 pigeons in 100 shots. I issued a challenge in the *Chicago Tribune* to any man in America to shoot a pigeon match for $5,000 and was not accepted. Again, in the *Chicago Tribune* I challenged any man to shoot prairie chickens against me in the field for one or two weeks, and winner to take stakes and all game. None of these challenges were taken, nor was my bet of $100 against $500 I could kill 100 snipes in the field without a miss.

I have made the highest records ever made in the world and general odds are now offered of $100 to $10 that they cannot be equaled by anyone. I accomplished the greatest feat of my life as far as endurance, rapid shooting, and accuracy when I broke 5,500 glass balls in seven hours nineteen minutes, shooting at 5,854 and loading my own gun. After this match I was laid up for several days that were most painful.

I could go on *ad infinitum* to matches I have won and upon which I rest my claim to Champion Shot of the World. As I am fifty years of age, I issued a challenge last October 20 to all in the world, for I was not willing to retire until all who called themselves "champions" had a chance to capture from me the honors I had won. That challenge has now been published five weeks and since there has been no response, I hereby publicly withdraw with my medals, badges, and cups from the championship and leave the field to others with the hope the best man may win the coveted prize which proves there is so much in a name.

In conclusion, let me add that certainly expecting to have my challenge accepted by noted shots, I secured a new W. & C. Scott & Sons gun for this special match. But as I have not been forced to it in my retiring challenge, it will serve me well in the spring when as a partner of the Hon. W. F. Cody I will go on the road with the Buffalo Bill Wild West Show. I will be accompanied by my four sons, aged eighteen, thirteen, eleven, and eight, and than whom no better marksmen of their ages live. I am with respect, Capt. A. H. Bogardus.

Although it was intended to be at the time, this was not Bogardus' swan song. His fortunes with Bill Cody consisted of bad luck and bitter disappointment. He had invested his own money, which he watched go down with a steamboat carrying the show's equipment and animals.

It wasn't until July, 1888 that he formally retired, taking with him the championship trophy, and leaving behind none emblematic of the Championship of the World. Manufacturers then placed several in contention, but all had to be won under special conditions. Dr. Rowe then donated the *American Field* Cup, which from that date forward was considered the World Championship trophy.

Bogardus' last recorded match on live birds was in 1898 at Hot Springs, Ark., where he operated a shooting gallery. Though still quick of eye and skillful enough to kill seventy-six of his 100 birds, he was not the same man as in 1879 when he and his arch rival, but close friend, Doc Carver, agreed to the match of the century.

This was a meeting of the giants and what the shooting public had long clamored for. The two men met at the Astor House to determine the conditions of their great match. It was first talked of a 1,000-glass ball shoot, but this was abandoned and in its place was proposed the most severe test of shooting skill and endurance then known.

The conditions provided that each contestant would break 20,000 glass balls within six days or 144 hours. They were to be sprung from two Bogardus traps at fifteen yards rise. The match was to be shot between September 1 and December 31, 1879, the stakes to be not less than $10,000 per man, and as much more as could be mutually agreed upon. The match was also to be thrown open to all comers, each contestant, however, to deposit a sum equal to that of Carver and Bogardus. The winner to take all gate money plus aggregate stakes.

The rules and dates were given to the press and it appeared all arrangements had been made when Dr. Carver remembered he was to sail for Europe with his backer, W. H. Huntley, and would not return until late in the spring or early the next fall. But Dr. Carver said, "I am very much in earnest in shooting this match at a later date and if I'm beat I'll slope for the prairies right off."

The truth of the matter was that both men were very evenly matched in both skill and endurance. Carver, almost as big a man as Bogardus, was six feet, two inches tall, slim, and in excellent health. It is doubtful that either was convinced he could out-shoot the other. Neither man had the amount of money agreed upon, and because they were so evenly matched, could not interest their backers in risking $10,000 at even odds.

Carver and Bogardus did shoot against each other in well publicized matches, but that were, in effect, exhibitions. They also toured the country together demonstrating the new flying clay pigeon and did much to popularize it.

Although he did so later, Carver would not for years shoot at live birds. He said, "Pigeon shooting is distasteful to me and my skill can be shown quite as well with a glass ball as with a pigeon." It was with the glass ball, often the Ira Paine feather-filled ball, that Dr. Carver gave his shooting exhibitions in theaters throughout the country. He used reduced charges against a heavy canvas backstop. A person was selected from the audience and taking a glass ball would throw it as quickly as possible away from the Doctor. In some theaters this meant as close as twenty-five yards, or as far as fifty or sixty. He was seldom known to miss.

He organized a traveling tent show that was a forerunner of the Buffalo Bill Wild West Show and, in fact, Cody copied and used many of Carver's trick shots in his own acts — most notably, the breaking of glass balls from the back of a running horse. Actually, Carver and Cody started show business together when they opened at the Omaha Fairgrounds under the cumbersome title of "The Wild West, Hon. W. F. Cody and Dr. W. F. Carver's Rocky Mountain and Prairie Exhibition."

Carver's exhibition shooting was on a par with Bogardus', and his later work along these lines was done with a Spencer pump gun holding eight shells with which he would dazzle the spectators by the rapid destruction of as many as 1,000 balls in forty-one minutes. But this was with the thrower standing at his side and he seldom let a ball go further than five yards beyond him.

He was a great favorite, his shows booked solid, and usually sold out to capacity. He was also a good salesman. His spiel to the audience during shooting would be on the merits of his guns, shells, powder, and other equipment — all of which he was using under contract. But since this was not generally known, he was free not only to sell a company's product, but to make disparaging remarks against competitors.

This did not endear him to the shooting fraternity, but when through a gun accident he was thought to have been rendered permanently blind in 1887, he received many thousands of letters of sympathy from the public. The accident was caused by the head of a shell splitting, and Carver was blind for three days. A short time before, his regular guns had been stolen from him and he was using an older gun that, as he put it, "was unfit to battle longer." But Carver, always the prima donna, placed the blame elsewhere. He was now shooting Dittmar powder exclusively, supposedly. But from the hospital, he issued the statement, "I have been experimenting with Schultze powder and have come to the conclusion that it is a most dangerous compound."

And then he took out his ire on Henry C. Squires, the New York dealer and agent for Greener, saying that he had returned a gun to Squires for which he had paid $600, and that in exchange had been given "the cheapest-looking gun I ever saw." And when he asked for one of the better ones in stock, he said Squires told him, "You can shoot with anything." Carver added, "Socially, he is a good fellow and is doing an immense business."

A few days later, Squires answered him in an advertisement saying,

> It is true I refused to let the Doctor pick out the most expensive gun in my case in exchange for his old one, but only because he is no man to have a fine gun. As everyone acquainted with him knows, he shoots it very hard and then throws it down without wiping and never looks at it until he wants to shoot again. As to his accident, he persisted in shooting the gun although my gunsmith who took it apart said the main spring had been broken so long there was not the least particle of fresh steel visible, and one-half of it dropped out when it was opened. I do not like to see fine guns used that way.

But right or wrong, surly or not, Doc Carver was one of the best of his time.

Probably the only man contemporary with Carver and Bogardus that could shoot alongside them day after day for an even tally was Fred Kimble. While his personal fame rested more on his discovery of choke boring and being a great market hunter, he was a superb, all-around shooter, as much at home on the trap field as in the duck blind.

He was a talented and remarkable man in many ways, whether giving exhibitions of figure skating or violin concerts. He was known as being unbeatable at checkers, a game quite prominent and popular in his day. His inventive mind took him into many fields. He improved on and perfected the formula for clay targets, invented one of the most popular traps of the day for throwing them, and was instrumental in the development of that most important discovery — choke boring of the shotgun.

Accounts of his marksmanship and early days of market hunting have appeared in books and many magazines articles. Going over these printed accounts with the idea of sifting facts from fiction is not easy. In 1868 Kimble lived in Chillicothe, a town twenty miles up-river from Peoria, Ill., and having the advantage at that time of being located near some of the greatest mallard duck-shooting ever known. An area that led Van Campen Heilner to once remark, "When all the mallards are gone, there will be some left in the Illinois River Valley."

The late Major Charles Askins said, "There was nothing in shotgun shooting that Fred Kimble didn't know." Leffingwell said, "My good friend, Fred Kimble, is reputed, and I declare I honestly believe it, the finest shot at wildfowl in America."

Joe Long not only dedicated his book, *American Wildfowl Shooting*, to Kimble but made many mentions of him, along with publishing a part of his diary for the spring of 1872, and which showed a record as follows:

Feb.	27:	Killed	70	ducks
	28:	"	74	"
	29:	"	81	"
Mar.	1:	"	76	"
	2:	"	106	"
	3:	"	61	"
	4:	Didn't	shoot	
	5:	Killed	66	"
	6:	"	107	"
	7:	"	57	"
	8:	"	65	"
Mar.	9:	Killed	82	ducks
	10:	"	60	"
	11:	"	72	"
	12:	"	128	"
	13:	Didn't	shoot	
	14:	Killed	122	"
	15:	"	70	"
	16:	"	68	"
		Total	1,365	Ducks

A total of 1,365 ducks and five brant (not recorded) in seventeen days of shooting. All were taken with a single barrel muzzleloader of 9-gauge. Not over three ducks were killed with any one shot.

At this time Kimble hunted with Henry Doty, of Henry, Illinois, and Alden Wilky whose name is seldom mentioned in old reports, but who must have been a pretty fair shot since Kimble said he was "the best duck shot ever seen." It was Wilky's houseboat they used as a base of operations up and down the Illinois River. It was often anchored around Duck Island where Kimble remarked, "The wild rice was thick as a wheat field. No boat could penetrate more than a length or two into it." He said they would shoot until noon and put in the balance of the day finding and picking up dead ducks. At this time Kimble was shooting a double barrel muzzleloader built by O. P. Secor, of Peoria, and a single barrel 6-gauge.

Another indication of the vast supply of ducks, and Kimble's skill in bringing them down, was that by using a single barrel muzzleloader he had before nine o'clock one morning taken 122 wood ducks at Spring Lake.

In the book *Supreme Duck Shooting Stories*, published by William C. Hazelton, Kimble tells one time of shooting at Peoria Lake which was covered with bluebills feeding on still slops dumped from a glucose factory at the foot of Main Street. One morning Kimble set out about fifty decoys and the bluebills started coming in to the slops at daylight. He had boys stationed 200 yards down current to pick up ducks as they floated by. When the ducks would come within forty yards Kimble would rise and take them, making one run of fifty-seven straight with his muzzleloader.

He reports Peoria was then about 25,000 people and that spectators began to collect on shore at the foot of Main Street. The bank was lined with people, many of whom had never seen birds of any kind shot in the air before. Kimble's father was among the crowd and lived only a short distance from Main Street. He brought his son a dinner pail of hot oyster stew at noon, and Kimble then continued shooting in front of his appreciative audience, to further establish his fame, and later stated he thought it may have been the only time a market hunter performed afield for a gallery.

Throughout the towns and villages up and down the Illinois and Mississippi Rivers were men noted for their duck hunting and shooting skills. Each of these villages had their "champion," many whose fans thought him surely the most expert of all. And this belief led to the "duck matches." The champion from one town would visit another to challenge the local hotshot and the side bets ranged from the winner taking all game, to thousands of dollars. In the beginning the rules were simple — each man to shoot for a given length of time, and on their return the winner was the man who had the most ducks.

Kimble regularly participated in these matches, at least whenever he could find a shooter to accept his challenge. He said his most famous match was against Reese Knapp, of Browning, Ill. Knapp shot what was then said to be the biggest gun in Illinois — a 4 bore single barrel weighing sixteen pounds and customarily loaded with two and a half ounces of shot.

When Knapp saw Kimble's "little" gun and learned he was going to use only one and a quarter ounces of shot, he apologized to Kimble for the beating he was going to give him. Knapp, who was certainly the finest shot in his part of the country, did not know that the "little" gun was Kimble's famous Tonks-made 9-gauge with a full choke bore, and probably the only choke-bored gun then in Illinois. At the end of the contest, Knapp came in with thirty-seven mallards against Kimble's 128. Kimble said, "These matches were interesting to me then — more interesting now because nothing like them will ever be possible anywhere in the world again."

Kimble often remarked that "The price of good shotgunnery is constant practice." And from all reports, he followed his own advice by shooting throughout the year. But he seemed to care little for target shooting. Because of his great skill, many tried to talk Kimble into shooting live birds or glass balls with their backing and a split of the money, which on occasion he would do.

In the 1872 Illinois State Pigeon Shooting Championships he shot the only single barrel muzzleloader on the grounds, and this against Bogardus. The two had eliminated 149 men after both went straight at thirty-one yards. Bogardus then asked for a division of honors and money, to which Kimble agreed.

Kimble was backed by Rollin B. Organ against Doc Carver shortly after the Carver-Bogardus matches, but Carver would not accept. His principal backer was Dan Voorhees and for whom Kimble never lost a match. His long runs on glass balls were widely known — one of them 735 straight. And it was almost impossible for him to find a competitor who would bet money on even terms. My files show Kimble taking first or second in twenty matches. They were all shot against top men such as Budd, Stice, and Fahnestock. The targets thrown were the popular Peoria Blackbirds of Kimble's own design and manufacture. Even at the age of eighty-four, when living in Los

Angeles, Kimble regularly broke twenty-three out of twenty-five birds at trap.

The last recorded interview with Kimble of which I can find record was by Charles Roth, and published in the November, 1936 issue of the *American Rifleman.* This was during the height of our duck depression, which in reality was caused by a seven-year drought in the Canadian breeding grounds, but which many people blamed on the tremendous kills of the market hunters before them. Because of this change in public attitude and his advancing age, we may excuse Mr. Kimble for being quoted in this interview as saying, although he had known many commercial hunters, he had never hunted ducks for market himself.

Throughout his life, Kimble was an exception among top shooters in that he was possessed of a modest nature. He does not appear to have sought fame at any point in his career, nor did he exhibit the competitiveness of his contemporaries. Accounts of Kimble by those who knew him personally all used the term "gentleman."

Certainly there were many market hunters to whom this term did not apply, even though their hunting skill was great. An example, and somewhat typical of many names not often mentioned in our shooting history, is Jake Groat. He was chief hunter for Messrs. Knobloch & Price, the Chicago game dealers who did a large volume of business from about 1883 to 1887.

Groat's address was a houseboat on the Illinois River somewhere between Liverpool and Lacon, the exact locale depending on where there was the greatest amount of ducks at the moment. He was locally famous, or infamous, not only for his skill as a shooter but also for his often quoted boast that he could "kill 200 ducks and a bottle of booze a day."

He was a true poacher, and a dangerous one. He delighted in hunting private club lands and was seldom asked to leave by the caretaker whose job paid too little to risk a beating, or worse. He was a big man, surly by nature, aggressive and argumentive.

It is known only that he shot a 10-gauge double barrel with no record of maker or type, and that he often took part payment for his game in powder and shot, which he used in great quantity. He participated in many of the "duck contests," but it was said he usually entered under an assumed name in an area where he was not known. Few knowing him would shoot against him, not only because of his skill but because of the difficulty of getting him to pay should he lose. In later years, Fred Kimble was asked if he had ever shot against Jake Groat and he replied that he had not, but that he had known "good men who had and wished they hadn't."

There were many men throughout the country who made their living by the shotgun, becoming spectacular wing shots through constant practice, if no other reason. Their accounts were their own and the location of their shooting grounds secretive. They neither sought nor received publicity.

The "fancy," or exhibit, shooters did. They hired agents and publicity men whose only job was to see that their name became a household word, even though their actual skill was less than many unknowns. In some ways, this was true of one of the most famous names of all, Annie Oakley.

Her career has received extensive coverage through the stage, motion pictures, and books, few of the writers being shooters themselves or having real knowledge of what constitutes good shooting. This is not to say that Annie couldn't shoot. She could shoot well with pistol, rifle, or shotgun. Certainly far better than any one of her sex, but not nearly as well as many men of her time, or even her husband, Frank Butler, who realizing the greater salability of Annie's fame, relegated himself to the position of agent, rather than competitor.

Annie started shooting with a single barrel muzzleloading 16-gauge. She said her first "real" gun was a hammer Parker 16-gauge, and this was the gun she shot at the beginning of her career in Buffalo Bill's Wild West Show. It came with 100 brass shells in which she used Dittmar powder for a short time, but she soon fell in with the popular idea of the day that smokeless powder would not work well in brass cases. She went to Schultze powder in 1887, however, and from all accounts seemed to average about 40,000 shotshells per year. DuPont, the maker of the American Schultze, once published her favorite 12-gauge loads which on clay targets was three Drs. Schultze, one and one-eighth ounces 7½ shot.

The first mention I find of her shooting trap was at Al Bandle's Cincinnati club in 1883. By 1885 she was giving exhibitions on glass balls, and once broke 4,772 out of 5,000. They were thrown straightaway from three traps at fifteen yards rise.

The Oakley-Butler story is perhaps best covered by Walter Havighurst in his book, *Annie Oakley and the Wild West*, and her early career so widely known that we will not go into it here, except for short sidelights that also tell us something of attitudes between English and American shooters at that time.

Annie was a world traveler and honored wherever she went. Here is a letter from Frank Butler, telling about Annie's and his English tour in 1887:

> In regard to shooting and shooters here, I must say I have changed my opinion very much. We misjudged the English shots indeed. I must say that from the Prince of Wales down, Miss Oakley and myself have been treated with the greatest kindness. The London Gun Club conferred a great honor on Miss Oakley by giving her a handsome gold medal—that being the only medal they have ever given away.
>
> As for pigeon shooting, with all due respect to American marksmen, I never saw any until I came here. There are no pigeons in America to compare with the English blue rocks. They are very swift and strong and make many darts and twists during flight. They can also carry plenty of shot out of bounds which is generally about fifty or sixty yards. No shooter can use a gun over seven and a half pounds, and many of them have much lighter guns. The traps are always set so the bird will have the wind which is very apt to be a stiff breeze. The trap works to perfection. I have seen about 1,000 birds shot at and only two set on the trap.
>
> I used to laugh when I heard Englishmen say no one could kill 80 out of 100, but now I say anyone that can do that can make plenty of money by coming here. I have only seen or heard of it being done once since I have been here. Mr. Journee, a French gentleman, killed 86. But then he is one of the finest, if not the finest, live pigeon shots I have ever seen.
>
> As for betting, there is no limit to it. About a week ago a gentleman lost $7,000 in one afternoon and no one appeared to notice it much.
>
> The Gun Club's grounds are said to be the finest in the world and I do not think there could be finer. There is a very handsome clubhouse and a stone wall surrounds it. The admission fee to see the shooting at any time is $5.00, being high to keep a certain class out. The Hurlingham Club has very large grounds and is said to be the richest club in the world. It has a membership of 1,500 and several hundred applications besides. It includes places for polo, lawn tennis, and other games, all being inside a beautiful park on the banks of the Thames. The guns used here are entirely different from our American guns. All look very plain in the stock, but they

balance very nicely and all shoot a very even pattern but not so close as the average American trap gun.

The English makers we hear most about in America are very little known here, with the exception of Charles Lancaster. He has a great many guns in use here. He is the inventor of a four-barrel gun and also has what he calls a Colindian gun made for both shot and ball out of the same barrel. I tried it and made a bull's eye at 100 yards with the ball; and then out of the same barrel I killed a pigeon at 30 yards rise with small shot. It takes about three months to have a gun made here. Nearly all makers have their private shooting grounds located in the city.

All shooters here use the smokeless powder in first barrel, especially Schultze and E.C.; black powder in second barrel, and mostly Curtiss and Harvey.

Many remember the boast of Mr. Dougall, of London, in which he said, "Ten English shots using 12-bore guns could beat ten American of equal skill using 10-bore guns." Of course, the Americans, I as well as the rest, laughed at the idea of such a thing being possible. But since I came here I am inclined to think he was nearer right than we gave him credit for being. I doubt very much if there are ten men in America who could come here and do it at the best blue rocks because the English 12-gauge guns, being light and well-balanced, handle very quickly and well, not letting a blue rock go far. Yet, on the other hand, I do not think ten English shots could go to America and beat ten Americans, because our birds are much slower there.

Every country has its shooting wonder and England is no exception. I had the pleasure of seeing Master Charles Brown shoot on several occasions. If he ever goes to America, which I believe he intends doing, all will think he is a wonder. He is a bright, gentlemanly, little fellow not yet thirteen years of age. But make no mistake, he can handle a gun.

Charles Lancaster, the famed English gunmaker, was very impressed by Miss Oakley, and not only spent much time instructing her and her husband at his private shooting grounds, but also designed several guns he thought best suited to Annie's style of shooting.

He found her regular gun had $2\frac{7}{8}$ inches drop at heel and no cast-off. The guns he built were much straighter, with $1\frac{3}{4}$ inches drop and a cast-off of 3/16. The first 20-gauge he built for her weighed $7\frac{1}{2}$ pounds and although they were lighter than the guns she had been using, he still felt them a handicap. He then built her a pair of 20-gauge breech-loading hammerless guns weighing only six pounds fourteen ounces each, which she used throughout her English exhibitions with great success. Another gun Annie made famous was a Sauer presented to her by Buffalo Bill and inscribed, "To Annie Oakley, little Missy, from Col. Wm. F. Cody, London, 1890."

But there is no doubt Annie was good with any gun she picked up. On her fiftieth birthday, she broke ninety-eight out of 100 at trap. Like other famous exhibition shooters such as Capt. Hardy, Kenneth Lee, Johnny Baker, and Frank Butler, she was more of a snap shooter than aimer — this style having been developed by her husband, who was one of the early greats of "fancy" shooting. He developed the shots on which the exhibition shooters' fame was built.

He was probably the first to use a black velvet backdrop on which were pinned black balloons inflated to about six inches in diameter. On these were painted small one inch white spots. From a distance, the outline of the balloon was invisible, but the white spots could be seen. Using a repeating rifle, it was not too difficult to rapid-fire ten balloons. A shot anywhere within six to eight inches of the small white spot would make it vanish. The much-applauded stunt of shooting rifles upside down also involved no great problem; the shooters simply held at twelve o'clock instead of six. But it was good showmanship.

Mostly what was involved in the shooting feats of the great crack shots of the Golden Age was not showmanship, however, but just plain astonishing skill. There were so many outstanding shots, whether at live or clay targets, in the theater or in the field, that it would take another entire volume to even begin to do them justice. But though their own extroadinary human skills deserve most of the credit for their shooting feats, some measure of credit must still be attributed to the remarkable evolution that took place during the Golden Age with respect to the hardware they used. And that, too, is a story in itself.

CHAPTER SEVEN

Breech Loading and Barrel Choke

IN BASIC principle, all major features of the modern form of dou-ble-barreled shotgun already existed by 1850. Even by then, exam-ples of the hammerless breech-loading action existed, as did self-ejec-tors, central-fire cartridges and choke boring. The superiority of these refinements, largely the achievement of English gunsmiths, seems so self-evident today that it is hard to imagine any serious reluctance on the part of nineteenth-century shooters to accept them.

Such, however, was the case. For twenty years later as the Golden Age began, one of the liveliest and most bitterly argued con-troversies indulged in by the shooting fraternity was still the relative merits of the muzzleloader and the new-fangled breechloader. One of the most popular books of the era, *The Dead Shot*, written by an author who called himself "Marksman" and first published in 1860, presented the case against the breechloader in these terms:

> Great credit is due to inventors of the breechloader for hav-ing succeeded in producing a very handsome and useful gun for short range; beyond that, no corresponding advantages are gained

by present inventions. The strenuous advocates of the breechload system, as applied to guns, have failed in their attempts to prove the advantages are equal to those possessed by the muzzle-loader. I have no wish to discourage those who possess breechloaders; they will find them useful for every purpose but wet days and long shots. As regards myself, I use a breechloader for tame game and in early season. But for all purposes of wild game and real sport, long shots, and security at the breech, I prefer a muzzle-loader.

Surprisingly enough to us now, these sentiments seem shared by the majority of shooters in that day. Then, as now, the average hunter was more concerned with shooting than the technicalities thereof. Again, there were a few people vitally interested in the improvement of guns and interested enough to compare and remark on the means of construction and matrials used. But the vast majority simply wanted something to shoot, leaving all thought of improvement up to the gunmakers. Since they knew nothing better, they were quite content with the equipment with which they were familiar.

The science of ballistics entered the subject less strongly than opinion, and the majority opinion held that the breechloader would not shoot as strong, nor kill game so far away, as the muzzle-loader. The newer gun was heavier, more expensive to buy, and used costlier ammunition.

It was widely believed that early breechloaders didn't last as long and needed repairs more frequently than the muzzle-loaders. It was said recoil was heavier and the sound louder, that the wetness of rain, fog, and snow could creep between the false breech and the barrels. And it did — often onto the shell itself, making the thin paper stick to the barrel.

There were claims of heavy vibration in firing, and stories of bursting by reason of gas escape between the breech. There was the time and trouble, as well as the danger, in filling shells. As one writer said, "The loading of shells to the sportsman is dirty and tedious; laborious as much as making fireworks."

Probably the most frequent complaint was the difficulty of carrying enough ammunition for the day's work. Since the businesslike hunter might be expected to fire 200 to 300 rounds a day, this many fixed shells took a great deal more room to carry than bagged shot and canistered powder for the muzzle-loader. The fixed ammo had to be carried in a strong case with individual compartments for each shell.

Rounds could not be carried loose without danger of damage. And in the case of pin-fire shells, they were quite dangerous to carry in the pocket.

Then too, since the shell was to be reloaded, it had to be withdrawn from the breech and replaced in the box for later use. And while the makers claimed the shell could be refilled two or three times, resizing was unknown. The shell expanded on firing. It was hard to rechamber on reloading and often stuck so that the copper end was pulled off on extraction and the paper casing had to be picked, or pushed out of the breech. Pin-fire loads were bent unless the hammers struck them exactly on center, and the pins would often fall out of reloads.

When metallic cases were used, 100 to 200 loaded brass hulls were a heavy and spacious load indeed. The muzzle-loader man carried his shot in a leather belt pouch, his powder in a flask, and his caps in a pocket box. Sometimes he would use metal tubes slightly smaller than the barrel of his gun. He would make these by placing the tube on a table and pushing a wad to the bottom. Then after filling the tube with shot, another wad would be placed over the top.

This way he could load the gun with powder in the field, place the metal tube in the muzzle of the gun, and quickly ram out wads and shot for fast loading. He would carry only two or three of these tubes filled and ready, and then reload them during dull periods so as to be ready for fast shooting. And the man equipped with these loading tubes boasted he was as fast in recharging his muzzleloader as was the man with the new-fangled breechloader.

Then too, while the trip to the hunting fields was by wagon or horseback, much walking was involved in getting to camp so that the breech-loader man carried, not only his personal gear but large, heavy boxes of fixed ammunition. Once there he sat up nights reloading his shells by lamp, fire, or candlelight while his muzzle-loading friends went to bed.

Another dissatisfaction with the breechloader was that the muzzle-loader was loaded for conditions as encountered. If the birds were flying high, light loads didn't do, but if they were working close why waste powder and shot with heavy loads? The muzzle-loader man could load for his requirements, while those who loaded light or heavy for their breechloader the night before were at a disadvantage. Since this objection was often quoted, it might lead one to wonder why, while loading, both light and heavy charges were not made up, but it was not the custom.

So, while some were willing to accept the breechloader as a superior form of gun, many were not. And it was believed that the chief, if not only, advantage was that it could be quickly reloaded. Even the most avid fan of the muzzleloader would admit no matter how fast he could load, he missed a great many chances at game while so doing.

Those defending the newer system were quick to point out the ease of cleaning and safety factors. The breech-loader man needn't have his hands and head over the muzzle at any time. This is where a great many injuries occurred. Most used in cleaning a muzzle-loader was a piece of flannel called a "tow." Great care was needed to see that no part of this was left in the barrel to be ignited on the first shot, then left to smolder. When the shooter was loading directly after shooting, the burning "tow" would explode the powder as it was dumped into the barrel, also lighting the canister of powder and perhaps blowing off a hand, eye, or head.

The man shooting a breechloader was in no danger of getting two loads in one barrel in the fury of hot and heavy shooting, and when the day was over he had to neither shoot off his loads nor withdraw them. He didn't carry ramrods, load rods, shot pouch, powder flask, or cap holder. There was no need to remove the caps when going into a house or riding a wagon, nor was there any need for carrying dangerous caps in the pocket. This was never recommended, but was always done for convenience as caps come in a box hard to open with the teeth and one hand, while holding the gun with the other. There was no mean juggling in a rocky boat while loading the gun, and as fragile as the shells were, the powder was in a more pure and safer state in the fixed shotgun shell than when poured in wet weather from powder flask to muzzle.

If the hunter carried a variety of shells he could quickly change from light-loaded 9's while snipe shooting, to heavy 3's in case geese approached. And in the case of those claims that the breechloader shot itself loose, it could certainly be proven this was caused more from the gun being carelessly opened and closed than from shooting. These objections were heard and heeded by the better English gunmakers, and rapid improvement followed.

The invention of the breech-loading concept is most often credited to Johannes Pauly, of Switzerland, who was granted a patent in Paris on September 29, 1812. It was a lifting-breech, drop-barrel gun. Of course, many breech-loading designs are known to have appeared much earlier in firearms history, but it seemed they lacked a suitable cartridge. Pauly fired his gun twenty-two times in two minutes during a Paris gun trial — demonstrating remarkable speed over that of the muzzle-loader.

But while Pauly was a fine inventor, he seemed a poor business-man as well as something of a rogue. He not only traveled extensively but was much given to changing his name and assuming aliases. And as one writer remarked, he may have been something of a ladies' man — which is known to have caused sudden changes of residence and name by men before and since.

Pauly's idea was refined by Lefaucheux, but during this early stage the shells remained pin- or needle-fire. It was not until 1838 that Dreyse, who was to become famous for the needle gun, developed what was probably the first practical center fire system. From here it was only a question of evolution on the original idea. And the serious student of arms research can find enough variations to occupy himself a lifetime. Both the Lefaucheux and Dreyse were probably used as models by Lancaster and Daw to develop both actions and cartridges, the direct forefather of what we are shooting today. They did away with one of the greatest drawbacks of early breechloaders — the escape of gas at the breech. The pin-fire cartridge could never overcome emitting gas at the pinhole. Because of powder gases escaping into the locks and water seeping into them too, rusting was so common that some makers installed a "crystal window" in the stock so the owner could inspect his locks at all times for rust.

Almost as soon as a new design appeared in England, copies found their way to America, and the earliest reference I can find to a breechloader having actually been made here was one designed and made by Joseph Hayden, of Oxford, Ohio, in 1850. It was said to have been pin-fire, and while he had purchased the barrels in the rough from England, the action was of his own make and design.

One of the earliest American production models of a breechloader was made by a firm best known for its rifles — Ethan Allen & Co., of Worcester, Mass. It was a trapdoor action with false chambers, opening from the top. Two dozen steel cartridges and a simple hand rammer about six inches long came with the gun, which was said to equal best British workmanship and material. It was before its time and found little popularity or large production.

So most of the breechloaders in American hands were British-made, and these were improving rapidly to the point of acceptance by our better shooters. So much so, that by 1874 Capt. Bogardus was given to remark in his book, *Field, Cover and Trapshooting*, that,

> The breechloader is an invention of enormous value, and so much improved upon since its first discovery and application that its principle and construction for opening, shutting, and securing the breech itself the most convenient, safest, and best gun in the world. A few years ago many good sportsmen would have disputed this statement, and there are some who would do so now. It is, how-ever, founded upon large experience and many trials of the breech-loader in my own hands against the most vaunted muzzleloaders in those of other good marksmen. I was, for some time after breech-loading guns came out, of a contrary opinion, but results convinced me of my error. Results always convince reasonable people — that is to say a great preponderance of results.

Bogardus said that they put the shot closer and distributed it more evenly than the muzzleloaders, in spite of many claims that it would not. He said the breechloader will also shoot as hard as the muzzleloader provided you use a little more powder, and that his breechloading guns shot harder than any muzzleloading gun he ever tested them against providing he used a dram more powder of fine quality.

Now that the sportsman had accepted the breechloader, he vigorously fought against the self-contained striker mechanism, or hammerless gun. While hammerless mechanisms had been used on flintlocks in the seventeenth century, they were now thought of as a new fad — one that couldn't possibly succeed because no serious shooter would even consider it. How could you even tell if your gun was cocked? And every shooter worth his powder knew the hammers acted as a backsight to help bracket flying game.

It was claimed, with some truth, that the firing pin of hammer-less guns could not be made to hit upon the primer with enough strength. Most primers being as hard and uncertain as they were in those times, this was often a valid complaint.

While safety mechanisms had been worked out to the same degree as on guns today, they were little understood or trusted. The shooter before 1880 felt much safer with his hammers on half-cock. This prejudice was so strong that internal-mechanism guns were made with dummy outside hammers. And it wasn't until 1871, when Murcott developed the first true hammerless sidelock, that the concealed-hammer gun achieved any degree of success.

Shortly thereafter, a couple of resourceful gunsmiths in the employ of Westley Richards, Messrs. Anson and Deeley by name, obtained an 1875 patent for what is now recognized as the first really modern hammerless shotgun. This action continued to be made both here and abroad after the patent rights expired, and with only minor improvements is still being used in double gun construction throughout the world.

So from 1875 onward we had a breech-loading action that was basically as fine as any we can produce today. The same thing might be said of barrels as well, for as the breech-loading action was being developed and adopted, so, too, was the principle of choke-boring shotgun barrels.

Unquestionably, choke boring ranks with the greatest improvements in the history of the shotgun's evolution. Just why it took so long to come into general use is one of the oddest mysteries in shotgunning, for again, the principle seems to have existed for as much as a hundred years before it was rediscovered and then popularized during the Golden Age. Perhaps the explanation is simply that credence was given to the "ugly rumour" that choking would burst the barrel. Certainly this was believed by some, as witness this excerpt from Elisha Lewis' *The American Sportsman*, published in 1855 and reprinted many times:

> If the subtle fluid generated by the inflammation of gunpowder be suddenly compressed or checked by a contraction in the calibre of the barrel, an undue force is exerted on this point. This fact will of itself show the folly of attempting to increase the shooting powers of the gun by unequal boring of the barrel, or contracting of the diameter of the calibre at some given point in its length, as is practiced by some ignorant gunmakers. We cannot imagine any cause better calculated to burst a fowling-piece.

We don't really know who invented the choke. We can guess, and side with our favorite candidate, but we'll never know for sure. The whole history of the choke is confused by claims, counterclaims, and speculation.

In *Le Vieux Chasseur*, published in 1835, author Theophilus Deyeux writes of having seen choke barrels. There are references to a Prague gunsmith named Stanislaus Paczelt, who welded thin internal liners in his barrels as far back as 1730. W. W. Greener, in the first edition of *The Gun and Its Development*, published in 1881, tells us the Spaniards invented the choke about 1781 — in the ninth edition, the French.

In his *American Wildfowling*, Joseph Long gives the credit to a gunsmith named Jeremiah Smith, of Smithfield, R.I., and states that he choked barrels as early as 1827. But in 1882, a prize was awarded to W. R. Pape of New Castle, England, by a committee appointed by the *London Field* magazine to investigate the matter for his 1866 invention of the shotgun choke.

Mr. Greener himself writes of having developed the first *successful* choke in 1874, but we definitely know this was after Fred Kimble sent him a gun. It was also two years after J. L. Johnson of Young America (now Monmouth), Illinois printed a circular saying he was prepared to make anyone a gun that would shoot a full charge into a thirty inch circle at forty yards. Mr. R. M. Faburn patented a process for a recess choke in 1872, and there are examples of French guns made in the 1700's that have long, taper-bored barrels. Sylvester Roper patented a choke as an incidental to his revolving shotgun in 1868.

No matter who invented the choke, or had a patent or prototype to prove it, we must credit Fred Kimble in America, and W. W. Greener in England, with making known its possibilities. So let's hear from Fred Kimble himself — his version of how it came about, printed in *The American Rifleman* in 1936.

> I shot the first choke bore gun, so far as I know, in history. A gun which I had bored myself. It would outshoot any other gun in Illinois by thirty yards. In those days (1867) the greatest range any shooter could expect from this shotgun was forty yards. Mine would kill at sixty or seventy, and one of them at eighty yards.
>
> You may wonder how I happened to be the one to discover choke-boring when other men, for centuries indeed, had been working on the same problem. It was luck, blind luck; and more than luck, it was pure accident.

Even though according to some of my scholarly friends, choke-boring is mentioned in sporting literature as early as 1781, as late as the last quarter of the 1800's men plodded along with short range guns, cursing their inability to reach out and get more birds.

I don't know how the idea came to me, for I had never heard of these early experiments in choke boring; but one day I thought if I could constrict the muzzle of a gun — make it smaller than the rest of the bore, the shot wouldn't spread over so great an area. So I found a musket with a good heavy barrel and began experimenting with it.

I am no gunsmith, but I had watched gun-borers work, and thought I could do a pretty good job of boring a barrel myself. I bored it out true cylinder to start with and then fired it at a target forty yards away. It gave the usual shotgun performance — spread the shot over a five foot area. English gunmakers were experimenting with an idea of their own, of relieving the muzzle just a little, claiming that this helped to reduce the spread. I tried it and it worked. The spread was reduced from five feet to four feet but I was still not satisfied, so I bored the barrel from the breech to within one inch of the muzzle which I left smaller giving what is today known as a heavy choke. Then I assembled the gun (a muzzle-loader, of course), loaded it, and fired it at the target expecting to have my head blown off.

I went to the target not knowing what to expect but not expecting what I found: a seven feet spread of shot! That disgusted me, and convinced me that my idea was all wrong. I felt that as an inventor I was an excellent failure. And here is where pure accident enters. The gun being a muzzle loader, to bore it out each time I had to dismantle it by removing a plug at the breech; a long tedious job. When there was a chance of discovering something new I had the patience to do the job; but now that I was convinced that my ideas were fruitless, I wished to waste no more time than necessary. So I began cutting the barrel from the muzzle, intending to make it a true cylinder bore once more. As soon as I thought I had all the choke taken out I loaded up and shot at the same target from the same distance: forty yards.

Expecting to find the usual five feet pattern, I walked up to the target. But what was that? The entire shot charge was clustered within a thirty inch circle! This was the first target of the kind I had ever seen. I was excited. I thought, of course, that it was an accident — one of those freaks that sometime occurs in every field. I went back to the forty-yard line and tried it again and again with still the same thirty inch pattern. And then I knew I had what I was seeking — why I had it I did not know, but I soon found out. In running a rag through the barrel from the breech, I noticed that the rag would stick at the muzzle. In my haste reboring I had not taken all the choke out but had left just enough to do the trick.

I couldn't keep a thing of this kind a secret for very long; I had to tell somebody. My closest hunting friend was Joe Long, and I wrote to him. He lived in Boston and I sent him some targets. A letter came from Joe by return post demanding to know what on earth I had done to the gun.

Joe had just ordered a new gun from a gunsmith named Tonks so he at once changed the specifications and had it made according to my new wild idea. It was the first commercial job of choke bore, I think, in the world. It supported the theory, and shot closer than my experimental piece. Then I ordered a gun from Tonks myself — one he had started to build for a man who died before taking delivery.

This gun was a single barrel muzzle loader of 9 Ga. When it came to me it shot so close that for several months I was disgusted. Compared to the old open bored guns I had been using, this gun shot like a rifle, and I made more misses than I had ever made in my life before. Often I was tempted to give up the fool idea, but I didn't. I kept on shooting that gun, wasting powder and shot, until I mastered its use. Then I was in a class by myself, with a gun that had a range of thirty yards more than that of any other shotgun in Illinois.

The Joseph Long to whom Kimble refers dedicated his book to Kimble, but claimed the earliest person to whom he had been able to trace a knowledge of the choke was Jeremiah Smith, as mentioned earlier. Unfortunately, Long provides no evidence to support this statement. If Long had known of the choke from Smith, it would seem reasonable to expect him to have incorporated it in his own guns. However, it seems that he did this only after having seen one of Mr. Kimble's guns.

There is also some controversy as to whether Sylvester Roper was first, because of W. W. Greener's statement that his patent preceded that of Pape, the English claimant, by about six weeks — Kimble, of course, failing to ever file a patent. Roper's April 10, 1866, patent #53881 would not seem to cover the choke, only his revolving shotgun. It wasn't until July 14, 1868, that Roper obtained patent #79861 for a detachable muzzle device.

On balance, the evidence would seem to suggest that while Roper had knowledge of the choke, he was much more interested in developing his revolving shotgun. A faulty breech mechanism prevented it from achieving success, and Roper failed to follow through on the more marketable part of his patent.

W. W. Greener's chief role in the development of choke was clarified by Greener himself, who stated,

The author has never claimed to be the inventor of choke boring, although it is generally attributed to him. All that he wishes to say is that the form of choke he produced which has now been generally accepted and the method of producing it are of his own invention.

Mr. Teasdale-Buckell in his book, *Experts on Guns and Shooting*, amplified this statement in commenting,

> The introduction of choke boring may be regarded as W. W. Greener's greatest achievement. His previous inventions had shown his cleverness; this one made him famous throughout the world. Mechanism in a mechanical age like ours is not easy to grow famous upon. But choke boring as brought out by Greener in 1874 altered the whole system of gun boring and made close shooting the servant of the gun maker.

But by the mid 70's, no matter who invented it, the choke had taken hold in the public's mind and gunsmiths and makers were all busy. For, as "Gaucho" (A. W. DuBray) wrote,

> When choke boring first came out, the man who had nothing better than cylinder was unhappy in the extreme. For the man with the choke gun was relentless, cruel, and so selfish, that he lost no opportunity of displaying the marvelous performance of his improved weapon. The superiority of the choke bore was simply squelching.

And a careful study of correspondence to editors as printed in its day would seem to verify that only after Fred Kimble had made known the merits of the choke on his own guns was the public ready to accept the discovery. I am perfectly willing to go along with the late Major Charles Askin's flat-out statement that, "Fred Kimble discovered the choke in America."

The claim that Kimble's earliest patterns have never been bettered has led many a shooter to ask why. For explanation we can turn again to Major Charles Askins and his book, *Modern Shotguns and Loads*. The Major said,

Kimble's wonderful patterns were not only from his way of making a choke, or other people would have been able to duplicate it. . . . I have seen work of all kinds of clever modern gunsmiths, and not one of them could bore a gun which would put all its shot in a thirty inch circle at forty yards, not to mention all of the charge in a twenty-four inch circle, which Mr. Kimble sometimes did.

The truth is that Mr. Kimble had ballistic factors to work with that were superior to any we have now. He had a muzzle-loading gun of large bore; he used but one size of shot, #3, for his best results; and he had black powder of large grain, slow burning, but strong. He didn't have to place his load in a paper case and crimp it in; he didn't have a forcing cone to contend with, resulting in deformed shot as the charge was smashed into the true bore; and he didn't have the high pressures of smokeless powder.

Irrespective of these influences on density of pattern, our 1880 shooter did have the choke with its longer killing range, and the breechloader with its convenience — a gun very similar in mechanism and appearance to the best we can produce today. So any shortcomings now were not in the gun itself, but its loading. Many a $300 best grade gun was outshot by inferior arms because the "best-gun" owned didn't known how to properly load a shell. Before long, however, this problem, too, was to be solved.

[CHAPTER EIGHT]

Fixed Shotshell

A NEW breechloader was of little use to the man who had neither material nor knowledge to load a shell for it. Here was something infinitely more complicated and entirely different from pouring powder and shot down the barrel of a muzzleloader.

Most early breechloading manufacturers had metal shell casings made to fit their guns and sold along with them. Quite often they were primed. While the shells would last through many firings, they needed new primers for each shot and these could not be found on the shelf of a country store. The big city gun shop may have demonstrated to the buyer how the loading operation was to be done, but there were no printed instructions for use by the man on the frontier.

When the original metal casings split, ruptured, or became over-sized, it was often difficult to obtain new ones, even from the manu-facturer. Some models had a screw-off, or removable, head for primer replacement, the threads of which shortly became so corroded the case was worthless. A good example being the Draper, marked "F.D. & Co." and patented November 29, 1864. It contained a screw-down head and was known to explode in the hand of anyone careless enough to use too much pressure. It was later changed to carry Sturdevant's patented anvil.

The scene was further complicated by several systems of ignition such as pin-fire, offset, and central. Even when the central ignition system became most popular, the large variation in primers was quite confusing. Roper used at least five different primer types and shells to fit them. The casings themselves were made mostly of steel in the beginning, but some of brass, copper, or zinc. Uniformity between manufacturers left much to be desired. Some makes were known as a loose fit and others so large for the gauge that it was often difficult to chamber them.

Many of these casings were imported. Among them, Daw's, England's first central fire cartridge, and also products of the venerable firms of Eley and Kynoch. But we were making them here too. And the small manufacturers were trying their best to fulfill the needs of the sportsman, as well as the gunmakers buying shells marked with their own firm name headstamp.

When the first paper shells appeared they were flimsy affairs, ruined by wetness, and thought not to withstand shooting pressure as strongly as metal. The experimenters were busy, as usual, making penetration tests and writing to the journals to make known their results. It seems the universal conclusion was that brass *did* produce a harder hitting load. In the long run, brass was less expensive than paper simply because it lasted longer. By 1884 Winchester was offering paper shells in two and five-eighths inches 12-gauge at $11 per thousand, while the same gauge and length brass shell was $10 per hundred.

Adding to the confusion, the handloader now had both brass and paper and for which he used different primers and methods of crimping. However, this was nothing compared to the problem of the manufacturer who found he must offer the complete array of systems, primers, shell casings, and gauges unheard of today.

Although these ran from the cannon sized 00, 0, 1, 2, and 3, I believe we should consider the 4-gauge as the largest true shotshell. For all practical purposes, gauges larger than No. 4 can be considered as made only for yacht cannon, saluting, or punt guns. Even then it is doubtful that the American made shells in these large gauges were ever really intended for punt gun use. Some makers listed them in their catalogs at various times, and we know Winchester made a quantity of 3-gauge to be exported to England. It has always been assumed these were intended for the punt guns that were quite popular in Great Britain. Even though the punt gunner did not always load his shells to full strength, often cutting their length for reduced loads, the American-made shells were too short to take the required volume of black powder and still leave room for shot.

Even when we eliminate gauges larger than No. 4, we find it, plus 6, 8, 10, 12, 14, 16, 20, 24, 28, 32, and 36 gauge. Then there were 64, 55, 44, 9, 7, and 5 mm. The really odd and rare gauges were 6, 9, 11, 15, and 18-gauge. While all are known to have been listed, examples of some are not known to exist in collections. U.M.C. made an 18 gauge marked "Nitro Club" and also catalogued a 15-gauge, which leads us to ask what brand of gun were they made to fit?

The metallic case was *king*, but many experiments were being made with other materials. Marston & Goodell were on the market in 1852 with what must have been a limited production cartridge using paper for the shell and leather, or *gutta-percha*, for the base. And this is the last we heard of it.

We were importing paper shells from England by Lancaster and Needham, but I can state on reliable authority that C. D. Leet, of Springfield, Mass., was the first to make the paper shell in America. He was closely followed by the Delaware Cartridge Co. and U.M.C.

It was but a short time before everyone got into the act with either casings of their own manufacture or made by others with their private brand headstamp. This situation is one which even today fascinates the shotshell collector, yet limits his number by the sheer confusion of known names, but great rarity of actual cartridges.

Now, two new industries were born, that of the case maker, and that of the shotshell loader. The latter was usually a gunsmith or proprietor of a sporting goods store. Unless his loads were particularly renowned for one reason or another, his geographical area of business was small. But because he had knowledge, tools, and access to components, he could load and sell shells to the sportsman who had purchased a breechloading gun but, for one reason or another, could not, or would not, load for it.

Still, the average hunter tried. As soon as he had the foggiest notion of the amount of powder, shot, and type of wads needed, he commenced to make his own ammunition. Since neither black powder nor shot had changed from muzzleloading days, we may now speculate as to why he found it so difficult. But there are hundreds of examples in print that he did. While fine English-made black and pink-edge wads were available, the average man seemed to get by cutting his own from leather, felt, or what-have-you.

The typical hunter was dumping in powder, using a stick to poke in wads, and leveling off shot to where he felt enough paper or brass was left for the type of crimp he desired. The most prevalent manner of crimping was simply to place a top wad, fold in the paper, turn the shell over on a flat surface, and give it a sharp rap by hand. As may be guessed, this gave less than the desired results. Brass often was not crimped, just an over-size top wad holding the shot. The use of water-glass was a later development.

It was not long, of course, before implements were designed to assist the handloader with his then laborious chores. While probably pre-dated by the English Erskine "machine" and perhaps Powell's block, Edwin Schenck, of Baltimore, marketed here his popular Eclipse loader. It was simply a block of wood drilled shell size to hold fifty cases, with sliding trays on both top and bottom. The under tray was filled with primers and the over tray with powder. By judicious moving of both, the shell could be primed and powdered in one operation. Crimping was done with the shells in the block, and the paper rolled over with a device looking much the same as a brace and bit.

There were English-made cappers, recappers, and crimpers of the same design as today. But it is not widely known there were progressive-type loaders made in America as early as 1876. Camp's Automatic Cartridge Loader, manufactured by Camp & Wise, Stoughton, Wisc., came on the market that year with a price of $6. It could load both 10 and 12-gauge metal or paper shells of any length, each shell being charged and wadded in one operation, but crimping done separately.

By 1880, there was the Belcher loader, very similar in appearance to today's tools in that it was lever actuated and had large half gallon jars for powder and shot containers. Two years later we had a truly progressive machine in the Acme Cartridge Loader. It fed wads, powder, and shot for 100 shells and had a crimper attachment.

The Bridgeport Gun Implement Co., another Schuyler, Hartley & Graham enterprise, brought out the Rapid Loader and Crimper which stated in its advertising, "Shells promptly loaded in best manner. 100 in seven minutes." It cost $15 in any gauge, and was almost identical in appearance and operation to the loading tools on the market today.

For one reason or another, these machines never achieved popularity. There is little mention of them other than the advertisements, and we find the accepted loading tools were of single stage. The majority of these were manufactured by Ideal who started business about 1883 in New Haven, Conn. under John H. Barlow.

By the early 1880's, the popularity of metal and paper casings seemed about equally divided. There had been great improvements in both. The paper case was now becoming waterproofed by having been shellacked — a practice first started by Mr. Von Lengerke.

The brass case was going through many changes of design although some of these were utter failures; such as a very thin brass shell brought out by Kynoch and advertised to be of less weight for the shooter to carry, and accepting a larger charge in the same length shell. But they were so thin that unless each was carried separately they became useless by being bent and dented in the pocket. The opposite extreme was the so-called "everlasting" brass shell which was thick, heavy, and could not take a normal charge.

Geo. E. Hart & Co., of Newark, N.J., offered a nickel cone metallic which claimed many advantages and used a quote in advertising by Capt. Bogardus who said, "They suit me better than any I have ever used." But the impact of that statement may be tempered by the knowledge that Hart & Co. was at that time the manufacturer of the Bogardus trap.

U.M.C., who made both styles, started pushing the paper case and advertised, "By repeated experiments and great outlay for improved materials and machinery made for the purpose, we can now warrant our brown paper shells equal to any. They are sure-fire and will not burst in the gun."

Some of this great outlay had been spent in obtaining the loading machinery of C. D. Leet, actually bought in 1873 but apparently not put to use for some two years. Historians writing of the U.M.C. organization have written this machinery belonged to "C. D. Wells." However, this was a typographical error that appeared in a book of company history commissioned by Remington in 1912.

Now that the handloader had gone through a sorting-out period and could freely make his choice between metallic and paper, he was confronted with a still greater choice to be made. The "wood" powders had appeared — both smokeless and semi-smokeless.

To the average handloader, the advantages of nitro powder were offset by the loading problems it introduced. The English had the jump on us, as usual, in that Eley was producing a primer made especially for the new propellant. We tried getting along with our black powder primers and had sorry results. So much so that it became the custom for the loader to use a tube about the size of an ordinary lead pencil which he placed inside the shell and around the primer pocket — this to be filled with about 12 grains of fine-grained black powder. The tube was then left in place while smokeless powder was filled around it. The tube was then removed and the shell wadded and loaded as usual. By using this method, almost any primer gave sure-fire ignition to the new nitro powders. What it did to chamber pressures is not recorded.

The shell case manufacturers jumped at the new trend by using the name "Nitro" or "Wood" headstamped on the same casings they had been producing for black powder. But the new powders also necessitated new devices for loading. Our first pressure rammer was made by Bridgeport Gun & Implement Co., and was so constructed as to exert a uniform and steady pressure of nineteen pounds to firmly seat the wads. It was also furnished with extra springs to equal twenty-five and thirty pounds.

The difficulty of loading nitro powders by the individual further increased the demand for custom loaded shells. Montgomery Ward's Chicago store was selling over one million rounds of handloaded shells per year, and the loading was supervised by no less than Rolla C. Heikes himself.

Henry C. Squires had Frank Lawrence in charge of its Loading Department, and was selling cheap paper cases with DuPont smokeless at $19.40 per thousand. They also sold the Winchester Leader shell with better wadding, at $24.50. The best imported English shells were selling from $32.50 up. But 12-gauge shells loaded with nitro powder could be bought as cheaply as $16.00 per thousand, most especially in the cheap "Diamond" case, made for one-time use only by Delaware Cartridge Co.

So great was this business that custom loading firms began to appear in great numbers. Many powder and shot manufacturers set up special loading departments or formed firms under other names to offer loaded cartridges. The Chicago Shot Tower Co. started the Blatchford Cartridge Works in Chicago to produce a shell called the "C. [probably standing for "Capt."] A. Bogardus." Kynoch contracted with Henry C. Squires, of New York, to custom load their casings for American use, and these shells were sold in large volume. Von Lengerke & Detmold, the famous New York sporting goods dealers, set up a large custom loading department with the help and blessing of U.M.C. These firms, among many others, made standard over-the-counter loads of their own specifications, but did an equally fine business in a truly custom shell, loaded according to the desires of the buyer. These sometimes took strange forms, such as the "Hummer," a spiral spring inserted in the shot to produce a spreader charge, so named from the whirring sound it made on discharge.

H. H. Schleber, of Rochester, N.Y., offered a take-off on the Eley wire cartridge with his thread-wound long range shell, the shot charge being contained in a two-piece tin cannister, and the container supposed to open at fifty, seventy, or ninety yards, "giving close pattern and great penetration."

The high density magnum shell of today with its filler of polyethylene granuals to prevent shot deformation and increase pattern percentage was anticipated by the early custom loaders who filled the space between buckshot with sawdust.

Frank Chamberlin's invention in 1883 of a truly automatic loading machine — the start of the factory loaded shotshell — did not seriously hinder the custom loader for over a decade after its appearance. At least, it did not in terms of sales. The custom loader's problem now was in obtaining cases and primers from the large manufacturers who by now were producing factory loaded shells.

Several of the large firms, Winchester and Union Metallic Cartridge among them, had formed the Ammunition Manufacturer's Association. Its avowed purpose was to "secure uniformity of products." Since the AMA controlled primer and case making, they could decide who was to be favored or discouraged from selling loaded ammunition. Starting or existing companies large enough to pose a threat to AMA members were simply told that primers and cases were not available. The smaller outlets and individuals had little difficulty in obtaining primed cases. So they continued to enjoy a steady business from the trap and live bird shooters until the close of the century.

By then, the factories were offering a staggering choice in powder, wads, shot, and cases. It is estimated over 2,000 combinations could be furnished. With these factory shells readily available from the general store, the individual began buying rather than loading his own. Handloading of shotshells went into a decline, reached a dormant stage where it was to remain until revived in the late 1950's as a money-saving hobby for the trap and skeet shooter.

CHAPTER NINE

Powder and Shot

BEFORE smokeless powder came along, you had to shoot, and then duck down and peer beneath the smoke to determine whether or not the target had been hit. It was an accepted fact that when a gun was fired you could expect a great deal of noise and a greater amount of smoke, for this was characteristic of black powder, and black powder was *the* powder until well into the 1880's.

True, a few smokeless powders were available in the 70's, but only the more knowledgeable and daring experimenters had much to do with them. One of these was Arthur W. duBray who, writing as "Gaucho" said in 1879,

> I lay particular stress on using smokeless powder as when this kind, in light loads, is used, the shooter can tell at once where his gun is pointed, even in the act of discharge; while, what with the noise, smoke, and recoil incident to the explosion of black powder, it is extremely difficult to locate both gun and object aimed at — in fact, it can't be done by any but a person of great experience.

But there *were* shooters of great experience, and black powder in its better grades was generally thought to be far superior to the few brands of smokeless powders available.

For many years, black powder had followed the same formula, with slight changes by different makers. A basic mixture was seventy-five per cent potassium nitrate, fifteen per cent charcoal, and ten per cent sulphur. Since the speed and strength of powder depended on the quickness of the burning, its strength was regulated by the size of the grains. Large grained powder was known to be much cleaner than fine grained, and produced less recoil because of its slower burning. This rate of buring was also controlled by a glazing process which gave it a beautiful gloss, and because if its appearance alone, was favored over unglazed.

The favored method of testing the quality of black powder was by rubbing it on the fingernail, or between the fingers, to see if there was a gritty feeling. While this actually meant little or nothing, it was thought to be the thing to do.

There was also great controversy over which of the black powders burned the cleanest. John Bumstead wrote in 1869,

> Much is said about one powder being cleaner than another. Possibly there may be some difference in this respect, but hardly to that extent which many sportsmen imagine. All, at the very best, is dirty enough to satisfy the most slovenly person that ever pulled a trigger.

While our American powder makers such as Oriental, DuPont, Hazzard, and Orange were producing excellent powders for their day, many still thought the English Pigou and Wilks, J. Hall & Son, and Curtis & Harvey were superior. In some respects they were, because the English had long recognized that a different formula was needed for very warm or very cold climates. They often used a great amount of sulphur for powders to be used in hot and humid areas, and it probably did perform better for Southern shooters than the American brands.

No matter where made or used, black powder was best stored in a closed tin box or cannister and kept in a dry place. Though all black powder was hygroscopic, the cheaper brands often substituted sodium nitrate for potassium in order to obtain a more powerful explosive. Unfortunately it also more easily absorbed moisture and was easily ruined by dampness; once ·it had been wet it never regained its strength on drying. While the more affluent hunter discarded powder which had been exposed to dampness, the average man usually spread it on an earthen plate and set in sunlight for a few hours to dry. Others dried it by fire, placing the plate on the back bricks of the stove, a small quantity at a time. And it was routine for powder flasks and cans to be held over a fire with their tops open to admit heat and let damp air escape before filling. For this reason, the Waterbury Flask & Cap Co. product was favored because of its large opening. While called by the shooter the "Waterbury quick loader," it could as well have been called the "quick dryer."

A great deal of this black powder was going into brass shells which were cleaned by immersion in a can of hot water and brown soap. And just as the smoke from shooting was accepted, so was the fouling left in the bore of the gun which was also cleaned by boiling water and much elbow grease.

By then Nobel and Schoenbeins produced a radical change related to Nobel's discovery of nitroglycerin. While both had found gun cottons utilizing the effect of nitric acid upon cellulose gave absence of smoke and solid residue, it was far too violent in composition for use in ordinary firearms.

It remained for the Germans to develop a nitrocellulose and produce the first practical smokeless powder for shoulder arm use. This was "Schultze," named for its inventor. Schultze had turned his attention to the use of wood fiber in the manufacture of powder.

"Schultze" was in the form of small particles or cubes of wood cut transversely from tree trunks. This cubed powder worked satisfactorily, its main drawback being the extremely hard ramming required. To overcome this, the company introduced a granulated form in 1880. It was even in grain and density, requiring no ramming. This development was in cooperation with the English government which as early as 1869 had formed a company to manufacture the "Schultze" in England.

It was not perfect yet. Damp weather weakened it and hot, dry weather made it overstrong. This was finally overcome in 1884 by waterproofing each separate fiber of the wood before it was formed into grains, the process being briefly as follows: Soft timber was selected and after being torn to fragments was chemically treated until all resin in the wood was extracted and only the pure cellulose remained. This was carefully dried and treated with acids after which a long course of purification was commenced. It was washed with cold, warm, and boiling water for over a month, until the nitro compound was perfectly free from all decomposible matter. It was then roughly ground and at that stage waterproofed. Chemicals to regulate the composition were then added and the mixture formed into grains. These were subjected to hydraulic pressure to regulate the exact density and finally dried and sifted.

Schultze made only one quality, one strength, and one size of grain. It was made in very large batches, each batch being many thousands of pounds. But the result was about seven pounds less recoil than an equal load of black powder in a 12-bore gun of equal weight. It was clean shooting, giving very little smoke, acted less corrosive on the bore, and was loaded in bulk exactly as black powder without ramming.

But with all its advantages it did not achieve early popularity either here or in England. In fact, it was banned for trapshooting at both Hurlingham and Wormwood Scrubs under the impression that it caused balling of shot.

It also required a different type of primer than those in common use for black powder. Regular black powder primers often resulted in misfires and Schultze was regulated to Eley's primers which were stronger than American primers and gave a deeper flash than most English primers then in use. Even so, there were frequent claims of hang-fires or delayed ignition and the shell exploding as the gun was opened.

But the more experienced shooter realized both the advantages and limitations of Schultze, and in 1887 the English firm had hired a well-known shooter named Graham to introduce it to America. Graham was an excellent publicity man, as well as shooter, and he attended the major tournaments to show his powder's advantages. One of his most spectacular and favorite demonstrations was to show how slowly and evenly Schultze would burn by pouring some in the palm of his hand, then igniting it. But one sticky, summer day, when his hand was covered with perspiration, the powder stuck to it and he was badly burned. This canceled further use of that particular demonstration.

But he was successful in setting up the famous firm of Von Lengerke & Detmold's, of New York, as the agency for Schultze in

1885. And they were given the much improved hardened powder. Prior to that time, the Schultze grains were softer and would mash under pressure, giving an uneven burning rate from charge to charge. The black powder era was on its way out in America. So much so that by 1891 the trapshooting organizations were suggesting that the black powder men be forced to shoot separately, and as a group.

But while all indications show Schultze to be the most popular and accepted of the new smokeless powders, it was much predated in America by other brands less successful. In fact, hundreds of small American concerns tried to enter the market with their own formulas and claiming this or that advantage over the competition.

The term "smokeless" was little used then. It was called "wood" or "white" powder, and in the early 80's it was not only scarce but expensive. Then, as now, cheats and con men hoped to cash in by selling homemade concoctions of equal parts of chlorate, potash, and granulated sugar. This was mixed with a little hot water to make a paste and then rubbed through a sieve to form granules before it hardened. Often a bit of graphite or coal dust was mixed in to dye the compound and give it the appearance of powder.

It made a highly explosive, but very unstable, mixture. It produced a detonation, rather than a controlled burning and many people were injured from both handling and shooting the substance. It was particularly dangerous when used in the cheap, ill-made guns belonging to youngsters and "sometime" shooters to whom the low price of this so-called powder appealed. Hands, fingers, and eyes were lost, and, in a great many cases, lives.

These home-brewed powders and any picric acid compound were commonly called "gold dust," a name that remained in the dark corner of many a hunter's mind and spelled early failure for a factory shell so unfortunately named in the 90's. These compounds gave a particularly vile smell and were easily identified by the knowledgeable shooter who usually refused to stand near anyone shooting them.

But the legitimate powder makers kept experimenting and seemed to find each additive to the basic smokeless formula would produce different results in the powder. Such things were added as sugar, ether, alcohol, arsenic, starches, pitch, camphor, magnesium, or seemingly whatever was at hand. Few of them gained ready acceptance from the shooter and most brands went quickly and quietly out of business.

[109]

Other good brands of wood powder were coming in from England, such as E. C., which was hard of grain, fairly waterproof, and used by the English trapshooter with great success. Walsrode was a gelatine powder of good repute, as was Coopalls, Empire, and Diamond. But the most famous of all in the late 70's and early 80's was Carl Dittmar's powder, first made by Neponset Co., and later by the Dittmar Powder Works.

Never did a product get off to a worse start. Almost immediately, reports came to the sporting papers of guns exploding through the use of Dittmar. There was a running controversy in *Forest & Stream* magazine between the years 1878 and 1879 on whether Dittmar was safe or not. The magazine took the position that it was, but gave equal space to those claiming it was not. They printed official denials from Dittmar himself, along with lengthy explanations as to why each particular gun had exploded and how Dittmar had played no part.

But the shooting hero of the day was Doc Carver, who suddenly let it be known to one and all that he was using Dittmar powder exclusively. Ira Paine, too, became a fan of Dittmar and even went so far as to have easel stands carrying a small sign saying that he was shooting Dittmar erected alongside his shooting stand.

Carver said he used Dittmar powder in his shells, loaded for him personally by Mr. Haines, his agent, and that he thought them completely reliable, but was very careful to see that the powder measure was tapped a few times until the powder settled evenly. He then used one Delaware fiber and one Eley's pink edge wad to fit tightly in the shell. Since Carver had previously enjoyed making a mystery of his exact shell components and was little known to utter a sentence of gratitude toward any product from which he derived no income, it may well have been that he enjoyed a favor or two from Mr. Dittmar.

But whether or not, Dittmar started gaining a market, fighting rumors it could not be used in brass cases and would not give penetration equal to black powder. The brand steadily increased in distribution and sales until suddenly the Dittmar Powder Works, at Binghamton, New York, exploded on April 21, 1881, destroying eleven of its thirteen buildings. But it was immediately rebuilt and Dittmar became a standard for the next decade.

The American Smokeless Powder Co. had several powders giving good results when dry, but all were badly affected by dampness — almost as much so as black powder. Duck, shorebird, and seacoast hunters soon found it was worthless a few days after opening, and although widely distributed, the company made little profit, and about 1887 sold their entire assets to Laflin & Rand. The name was continued and changes were made in the powder to give more uniform results.

Laflin & Rand were thought to have made a superior duck-hunting powder of great uniformity. It was molded by machine into a string and then machine-cut into grains, giving a more even product than those granulated and screened. L & R's most famous brand names started with the word "Orange," and all were known as Orange powder, not because of the color, but because L & R had acquired the old Orange Powder Mills, in New York.

But nitro powders brought the shooter more problems than were to be found in the burning of the powder itself. They necessitated new devices for loading, different wads, and stronger primers. And the primer question is one that probably delayed complete acceptance of smokeless powder for close to a decade. Because coinciding with the advent of smokeless powder the shooter was confronted with another question that perplexed him as much as his choice of propellant. And that was the seemingly simple matter of shot.

Today, we give little thought to shot, except for choosing the size needed for the game at hand. But the history of shot is a complex one. It went through many stages of development and its seems the first multiple shot used in a scattergun was known as "swan drops." These were cut from lead sheets in a cubed form and ran anywhere from 200 to 300 cubes per pound, depending upon how heavy-handed or precise the cutter may have been. As it became smaller in size, it was known as "hayl shot."

The first record of small shot was its use by German peasants, and it was made by cutting lead wire or lead rods, and then rolling between flat stones to give it a somewhat rounded form. It is said a sharp chap named Bill Watts, a plumber of Bristol, England, found he could get fairly round and small pellets by pouring molten lead through small holes in the bottom of a pan, and letting it fall into a water tank. This method ultimately led to the shot tower — a system still in use.

While a great many materials other than lead have been used, it was the principal metal from beginning to present. It is heavy and cheap. It doesn't groove gun barrels as would harder materials such as iron or steel. And it can be easily melted and formed into fairly round pellets. While this shape is not ballistically best, less air resistant forms present other problems, and we have settled for the pellet.

At various times, everything from iron to pebbles have been blown out the end of a shotgun, and many a lad with his muzzle loader found that hard soup beans were effective at close range, and much cheaper than lead shot. But shot for our story is lead, and in the beginning it was pure lead. But the Germans discovered what we now know as hardened or "chilled" shot. It received the latter name because the Germans actually blew cold air across the dropping shot to temper and harden it. Since that time, the desired hardness has been obtained by adding small amounts of arsenic, antimony, and other substances.

Even though the discoverers could prove hard shot produced better patterns, they had a hard time making their point to the shooter. Most hunters in the early 70's thought the softer the better. They worked on the theory that each pellet flattened out, expanded, and increased in caliber as it entered the game. They also knew by weighing a given number of pellets that soft shot was heavier than the new chilled, and, therefore, it could not possibly maintain momentum and carry the distance with penetration that soft shot did. This attitude carried over into the twentieth century, and chilled shot remained unpopular in the southern states until World War II.

So, as was the custom of the day, the experimenter made many tests to compare chilled versus soft shot. This unofficial testing became so popular that a standard of penetration became the pages of *Harper's* magazine, and when a shooter told another that a certain load with a certain size of shot went twenty-three pages, it was known immediately he was speaking of *Harper's*. Most of this controversy took place between 1878 and 1880. By the latter date it became apparent that the magazine test was not giving the desired results. It was destroying the shape of the soft shot to the point where its exponents were claiming that it was too hard and flattened their shot too much for deepest penetration.

A man named O'Neil, from New Rochelle, New York, patented a penetration tester that was immensely popular. It cost about $4, and was made of poster-size cards in a framework to keep them slightly separated. They were made of a pasteboard that would yield and allow shot to pass from sheet to sheet without completely destroying its shape. Pattern was of little concern during these tests. Penetration was the thing. And it was good that pattern or percentages were not paramount because the shot industry itself was mass confusion as to sizes. For one thing there was more shot to the ounce in chilled than in soft. For instance, 399 pellets of size 8 soft shot to the ounce, but 409 pellets of the same size in chilled. That is if a standard size No. 8 could be found.

Shot sizes ranged from No. 12 and dust, up the sizing scale to a single caliber ball. No two manufacturers seemed to agree on what diameter a certain number shot should be. The fact they were using both English and American shot further complicated matters. While our size No. 8 (.08) carried 409 pellets to the ounce, English New Castle No. 8 was 450. And while the English makers used New Castle chilled shot No. 6 with 270 pellets to the ounce as a standard for their tests and patterns, for one reason or another, our shooters and makers could not agree upon any certain shot size to use, and it ranged from No. 10 to No. 4. I have read one report where the tester used "dust" shot which normally carries 4,565 "pellets" and should have made a monumental counting job, even if it proved nothing.

The shot size problem was supposedly solved for America at the New York State Sportsmen's Convention, held in Niagara Falls in 1872. A suitable scale was selected for the various makers to abide by. It was agreed among them that this would be the industry standard and that shot would be numbered accordingly. They evidently left the meeting in complete agreement, went home and continued making shot in the same sizes as before. In any case, ten years after the convention agreement, No. 6 shot from Leroy & Co. was still 209 to the ounce; Tatham & Bros., 218; St. Louis Shot Tower, 299; and Chicago Shot Tower, 216. And just when it seemed that the compendium of opinion agreed that chilled shot was superior to soft insofar as less leading in the barrel, greater penetration on game, and more even patterns, there came the controversy as to whether chilled shot would in time shoot out a choked bore.

Ira Paine hoped to answer this question by having his Parker Bros. breechloader measured exactly by a Mr. Nason, an engineer of Lewiston, Maine, as it came from the factory in full choke, and then critically measured again after Paine had fired it 35,000 rounds with chilled shot. Mr. Nason's verdict was that the choke was perfectly intact, though this answer did not satisfy everyone, and we find the same question repeatedly asked in the sporting magazines for the next several decades.

Happily, choked barrels have withstood the test of time pretty well, and although chilled shot *can* finally make a cylinder out of a full choke, not many shooters live long enough to have to worry about it.

Chilled shot has always been the most expensive item in loading, and manufacturers have constantly sought substitutes. Even iron was tried, long before the present-day concern about lead poisoning in wildfowl from ingested shot. Nothing, however, has succeeded in replacing lead, and shot remains today, for all the research of the manufacturers, very much like that of the last century.

CHAPTER TEN

The Decline of the Double

WHEN the Golden Age of shotgunning began, the dominant influence on American shotgunning was unmistakably British. Not only had the British pioneered the sport of "shooting flying" and developed it into something approaching an art, but their beautifully refined, hand-made double-barreled shotguns set the standard of excellence the world around, and were used by almost all American shooters who could afford them.

By the end of the Golden Age, most American gunners were using a domestically made repeating shotgun, inexpensively mass-produced and arguably better suited to the rougher American shooting conditions. How this transition from British guns and influence to a more truly American style of shooting and equipment was effected is one of the major stories of the period.

Until the middle of the nineteenth century, America had been a rifleman's country. The smoothbore had existed, of course, all the way back to flint-lock days, but it was derided as a "squaw gun," used mostly for pot hunting, and the sporting properties of the shotgun were exploited by few. The American gunmaker of that era was primarily a producer of rifles, making only an occasional shotgun on a custom basis. So in the most part, the knowledgeable sportsman bought an English made gun. Not only was it usually superior in workmanship, but incorporated the most modern improvements. Even when the gun was American made, if it was of high quality it used English barrels.

Even in England, the sport of shooting driven game had not become popular until the second half of the nineteenth century. But by then the Englishman had for many years done his wildfowling, pigeon, and partridge shooting with a gun much superior in design than that to be found in other countries. The English sporting shotgun was handmade. Traditionally, the art of gun making was passed from father to son, generation after generation. The apprentice system was used, with boys starting a long career of gun making at ten or twelve, but not being allowed to actually produce an arm on their own except after years of watching and learning.

English guns started with a barrel maker who forged barrels, bored them, finished and fit them until they were complete. Then an action fitter would take a block of steel, and with his hacksaws, files and chisels work away until there was an action. The stock maker started with a block of wood, and with his rasp, chisels, and saws, started fitting it to the action. Then the master fitter would come along and put everything right with his files.

Until well after the Civil War, the Old World gun predominated in the hands of the New World sportsman. By 1870, however, our sportsmen were becoming critical of the English product. To begin with, a good quality English gun was expensive. Secondly, its fine engraving, exquisite checkering, and smooth finish seemed somewhat out of place in the rougher and more primitive ways of hunting in the United States.

So now our own gunmakers took another and longer look at the English product, then started copying only those features they found functional, building the gun to more rugged proportions and omitting ornamentation to lessen costs. By the 70's, the American makers were using machinery quite different from any known in England. It was also more expensive than the smaller English makers could afford, but it was allowing us to offer our own sportsman a gun better suited to his needs, and much less expensive to buy.

The machinery in question owed much to the inventions of Eli Whitney of cotton gin-fame, who first developed the concept of interchangeable action parts, and to Tom Blanchard, a Massachusetts tack-maker who produced a machine capable of reproducing gun stocks. The greater use of machinery in manufacture by no means made gunmaking a production-line process in the present sense. However, American manufacturers did manage to eliminate much of the rough work by having the parts cast, forged, and machined to a certain closeness.

Of course, this did not eliminate the role of the master fitter. The rough parts still had to be fit up by hand. So when we refer to machinemade shotguns, we are not talking about stamping and fitting as known today. The American shotgun was in every sense a handmade gun with simply much of the rough labor done away with.

Our early "machine-made" guns differed from the English product in ornamentation and finish — so much so it could be seen at a glance. They also differed greatly in price, and this had not only to do with the 35 percent import duties imposed on the English product in 1881. Our guns were plain guns, made more as a tool than as an object of art. They were a needed tool, and one designed to be used under American conditions afield, which differed greatly from the English. The main thought in the American maker's mind was to produce a rugged, dependable gun that could be shot with the same power and accuracy as any gun made, regardless of price. They were making guns for the hunters, not shooters. In other words, a gun used by a "shooter" in England, who had his gun bearer and was shooting driven game, received far less abuse than that of the American waterfowler who would go for days at a time in the field, subjecting his gun to the elements.

While the live-pigeon shooter was not impressed with the crude American product, and in many cases was well able to afford more elaborate arms for his afternoon's use at the traps, the rural hunter looking for game for market or his own table and subsisting on a few hundred dollars a year income, found the American shotgun definitely superior for his needs.

There was little engraving on our early factory guns and they were stocked in plain, but solid, woods. Almost all barrels were imported, there being few gunsmiths who even attempted to make their own barrels. These, in the beginning, were of the cheaper Damascus variety. Different grades of guns by the same maker were not thought of. There was one gun produced by one maker in one model, made as best he knew how. Consequently, a $75 American gun could often be every bit the equal of a $200 English gun so far as its actual shooting properties. And the shrewd English gunmaker was quick to realize this fact, as evidenced by the hurried appearance of cheaper grade English guns designed for importation to America. They were of a plainness and quality that could not find acceptance on their own shores, but because of price were readily accepted here.

Thus the Englishmen began losing a prime market for their guns, except in the highest grades. This galled the British makers, including Mr. W. W. Greener, who in his first edition of *The Gun and Its Development* made some harsh accusations. In speaking of American guns he said,

> The barrels do not fit into the breech action. To make barrels interchangeable, such nice fitting cannot be entertained; and, therefore, none of the barrels fit closely, but a margin is left so any barrel may fit easily. Neither does the face or the breech end of the barrel bear evenly and closely over the face of the breech action body. The commonest Birmingham guns must do this before they can receive the proofmark. . . . The strikers do not strike centrally upon the cap; consequently, misfires ensue. The cause of this is that the barrels of different heights and even gauges are fitted to breech actions of the same size. . . .
>
> The barrels are not straight, either inside or out. This is due to lack of skill in laying them together. The ribs are neither straight nor put on evenly. The boring is of the roughest, and the shooting accepted as it comes. The symmetry of the gun is spoiled in order that the work may be finished so far as possible by machinery. No attention appears to be paid either to the balance, lay, or general make-off of the gun. The wood and iron only bear against each other indifferently. The heads of all screws are rounded and countersunk, not filed flat as in guns of English manufacture. The slits of the screws lie at all angles. . . .
>
> In fact, the shooting arm produced by scheme and human machines calling for no thought or skill on the part of the maker is barely useful or sound. No public proofhouse exists in the United States, and to the American sportsman is the proving of the guns entrusted.

This was published in 1881 and, as expected, drew an immediate rebuttal from American makers. Gun writer Capt. William Keith was one of the first to take umbrage at these statements. He wrote,

Mr. Greener is wrong. His statements are not accurate, nor kind, nor just, nor true; and I say this with a good share of praise for that gentleman's finest guns, and with admiration for his successful business methods, shrewd, sugar-coated advertisements, and productive literary matter in particular. Mr. Greener will certainly find he has gotten into a bad fix talking in this loose, inaccurate way.

Now, all the Colt, Parker, Remington, and Fox guns are bored mighty carefully, I tell you. Not only is the boring done just right, but the shooting as a consequence is exceedingly good. It is a point always seen to right at the factory. American work is plain, but really of a high order. And I would like to see some of our gun houses challenge Greener as to quality and performance of low price, machine-made shotguns against cheap Birmingham handmade ware.

Now when it comes to really artistic guns at a good round price, you know the Americans don't attempt to make them. The great British makers have been at the business for years and control trade of that sort.

Greener wrote back from his St. Mary's Works in Birmingham, "Respecting my adverse criticism of American guns, no evidence is forthcoming to show that we have in any way exaggerated the faults of American machine-made guns. Our statements were made upon a thorough knowledge of the difficulty, if not impossibility, of producing a gun by machinery."

It was a controversy that could never be completely resolved because of evident truth on both sides of the argument. The average hunter bought more and more of the American product because it fit his purse. The professional gunner continued to use the best guns England could produce, and looked down his nose at the American-made gun. In the end, however, neither side could be said to have triumphed, for the double-barreled gun itself was to prove vulnerable, no matter by whom it was produced.

By the 1880's the American shooter was presented with an astonishingly wide array of guns from which to make his choice. He could have the most elaborate custom-made London sidelock or the cheapest pot-metal Belgian import. He could have single barrels or double barrels, or even three-shot "drillings" or four-shot "vierlings." Apparently what the market hunter wanted most was fire power. But if three-

and four-shot guns were what was wanted, the available models were not the answer, for three or four barrels brazed together were both clumsy and expensive.

For a while it looked as if a revolving shotgun would prove the answer. The concept derived from Samuel Colt's splendid handgun, and was applied to both rifles and shotguns. However, neither Colt's nor Sylvester Roper's revolving shotguns achieved much in sales or popularity, probably because of the excessive gas leakage between cylinder and barrel.

One of Roper's agents, Christopher Spencer, patented a tubular magazine shotgun when he was only nineteen years old, but it did not function correctly and he could interest no one in its manufacture. He was more successful with his lever-action rifle, patented in 1860, which he formed his own company to produce in 1862, and which became the outstanding repeating rifle used in the Civil War. Spencer never applied his lever action to the shotgun, but in 1866 he met Thomas Lane, who redesigned the feed mechanism of Spencer's original sliding, or pump action shotgun patent and enabled it to become a practical reality.

The sliding action as applied to guns was known as early as 1854, in Alexander Bain's British patent of that year, and rifles utilizing Bain's and other patents were made in both France and England. However, the Spencer Model 1885, based on his patent of 1882, is generally considered the first successful repeating shotgun of pump action. The rigid-frame Model 1885 was followed by a take-down model in 1887, and both of them appeared to achieve the market hunter's fire-power objectives. With either, the hunter could get off six quick shots, or three times the fire-power of the double barrel.

But again, this was a departure from the type of gun the average hunter had known, and the change was resisted by some as stubbornly as had been the breechloader and smokeless powder. The repeating gun was called a game destroyer, was said to be clumsy, would clog up, was difficult to use in snow and freezing weather or where fine sand and dirt was present. The pressure of the magazine spring was thought to bulge shells so that they would not chamber properly. But worse yet, it was charged that the man using the repeater wanted every bird in the whole covey and every duck in the flock, without thought of leaving some for seed. A gun writer of the day wrote,

> The pump gun is the pot hunter's tool. Nine out of ten men shooting a pump gun would delight in finding a covey of quail in a

ditch and potting them on the ground. How can a man use one of the vile things? I would as soon catch trout in a net.

A report in December, 1898, printed in the *El Cajon Valley News* told of a hunting party at Otay Dam. The item read,

> The sport began at 6:00 a.m. when the hunters entered boats on the reservoir and pulled from one end of the lake to the other. On the first trip over the water they brought down 700 birds — the trip occupying one hour and a quarter. Each man had two repeating shotguns and was thus able to shoot 12 shots without reloading. Two more trips were made over the lake, and the total bag was brought up to 1,502 birds.

This so infuriated California sportsmen's clubs that at the next meeting of the legislature a bill was passed forbidding the use of re-peating shotguns. This law was short-lived and struck down by the California Supreme Court, which said that while a state may place a limit on birds to be taken, it could not say what gun to use. If so — it might say all breechloaders were bad. We would then have to return to the muzzle-loading gun. So it was an uphill fight to convince the sportsman that the repeater was a sporting gun.

But the same sort of luck that brought Christopher Spencer to meet Thomas Lane also brought a similar meeting with the shooting hero of the day, Doc Carver. Carver had shot W. W. Greener guns for fourteen years of his professional career. These guns were all purchased through Henry C. Squires, Greener's New York agent. Carver had proudly claimed that neither Greener nor Squires had ever paid him one cent for using a Greener gun, and that if the Americans could ever produce a better arm, he would use it.

Just prior to his meeting with Spencer, Carver had a gun accident affecting both eyes. He and Henry Squires had had several disagree-ments and he was in a very receptive mood toward changing his brand and type of guns. Whether or not money changed hands in the deal between Carver and Spencer, we will never know for sure, but we do know that Carver expressed the desire to be able to say about Spencer what he had always said about Greener — that he had never taken a cent for using his gun.

But even in the old days there was more than one way of swinging a deal. Shortly after their meeting, Carver took a Spencer gun and broke 1,005 glass balls in 41½ minutes. He used three Spencers handed to him loaded as needed. For this feat he was publicly awarded $1,000 by Spencer. Immediately thereafter, Carver began a tour of this country and England popularizing the repeating shotgun, and his gun was a Spencer.

This is not to say that Spencer had everything his own way. In 1885 the Winchester Repeating Arms Company purchased the Browning brothers' patents for a lever-action repeating shotgun with a capacity of five shots — four in the magazine and one in the carrier — and successfully marketed this gun as the Model 1887. In 1892 the Burgess Gun Company of Buffalo, New York developed a shotgun which utilized a sliding pistol grip instead of a sliding forearm, and marketed it with some success.

In the end, it was not Spencer's slide action, or Browning's lever action, or Burgess' pistol-grip sliding action that destroyed for ever the double barrel's supremacy in America. It was the Browning brothers' response to Spencer's slide action shotgun, a slide action of their own having a visible hammer, side ejection and a tubular magazine holding five shells. The Browning action first appeared in Winchester's Model 93, but when mechanical weaknesses developed with the use of shells loaded with smokeless powders the gun was withdrawn, and a revamped and improved model, the Model 1897, was issued.

Success of the M/97 was instant, and the gun quickly outdistanced the sales of the Spencer and Burgess. More than a million M/97s were to be produced in the next half-century, a surprising number of which are still in use today by those who prefer a visible hammer. And the dominant British influence in American shotgunning at last was at an end.

Gunmakers of the Golden Age

FROM the 1940's until recently, gunshops took old double-barrel shotguns in trade only with the greatest reluctance. Such trade-ins were quickly relegated to some remote corner of the shop, to gather cobwebs until a buyer could be found for the princely sum of $5 to $10. Often these relics were sold for parts alone, for even the most ruthless dealer would hesitate to pass them off on customers intending to shoot them.

Gradually, however, nineteenth-century rifles and pistols became scarce and expensive, those wishing to collect arms turned their attention to the more cheaply and easily acquired shotgun. By the mid-1960's there was a frantic scurrying of shooter/collectors to unearth old shotguns by Parker, L. C. Smith, Ansley H. Fox, and other famous makers. Prices soared; a Damascus-barreled Parker available in the 1950's for $25 or less soon commanded four to five times that amount, and the new owner was often happy to spend another $200 to have it rebarreled in modern steel. Collectors, of course, considered it a sacrilege to even refinish the stock, and paid premium prices for original condition.

As prices continued to rise and the supply of guns by well-known makers dwindled, an interest in lesser-known makers of the Golden Age began to develop, and collectors began to seek out double-barrels of almost every age, condition and origin. And along with this resurgence of interest has come a pressing need for a compilation of all available information about such guns and their makers.

The author is well aware, of course, that the following compilation is far from complete or definitive; it is only a start. For there is little likelihood that any catalogue of double-barrel guns made or used in the United States before and directly after the turn of the century will soon be complete.

Reliable information about old makers is difficult to obtain. Few writers were interested in chronicling guns at the time when the facts and records were obtainable. Moreover, the government did not require extensive records such as those that must be kept today, and the gun manufacturer could consider his business his own. When a firm moved, merged, was sold or failed its past records were often destroyed or left behind.

Thus, much mystery, speculation and pure guesswork is involved, at this late date, in trying to identify the many hundreds of brands as to their actual makers and dates. Most of the information must be gleaned from advertisements of the day, newspaper clippings and vague references in books of the time. For few small gunmakers bothered to prepare a catalogue, and many considered their output too small to justify advertising.

The most serious obstacle facing the historian is that of private brands. It was a custom of the trade from the 1880's through 1930's for both small and large wholesale hardware and sporting goods firms to buy or import double-barreled guns in all grades, marked and identified only with the distributor's own brand name(s). The same identical make and model gun often can be found under a dozen different brand names. The most serious offender in this case was H & D Folsom Arms Co., of New York, but there were many others.

The editors of gun magazines constantly receive letters of inquiry as to who made such-and-such old double-barrel gun, its history, selling price, and value. These guns carry names such as "Crackshot," "Compeer," etc. Since several hundred different names were used on guns very much alike, most editors offer a stock reply,

Appendix A

Your gun was probably made between 1900 and 1930 for a hardware wholesaler under their private trade name. Since the name of the manufacturer is uncertain, the gun should be examined by a competent gunsmith before attempting to shoot it and guns with damascus barrels *cannot* be recommended for smokeless powder shells. The market value of your gun is probably less than $10.

This answer is used so often that most gun editors can type it in their sleep. It's the answer we use because we simply don't have enough information to give a more intelligent one. Of course, even knowing the maker's name doesn't help much. The value of these guns depends on many things — condition, grade, model, whether damascus or fluid steel barreled, and rarity. At this writing, there are established values only for guns of relatively famous makers, and the price for most of the others is simply a matter of what the buyer will give and the seller will accept.

This will change, of course, as the collector movement grows, and growing it is. In time, the names and history of more guns will be known and clubs and organizations will be formed to set price guidelines. In the meantime, it is hoped that the following compilation will serve a useful purpose. For all its shortcomings, it is the most accurate listing I have been able to compile after many years of research, and it is the most comprehensive one I know to exist. I very much hope that its publication will help to bring to light much new information, and enable me ultimately to correct whatever errors of commission or omission it now contains.

The guns listed below are only those believed to have been made or in prominent use between 1870 and 1900, give or take a few years. This will result in confusion if you do not keep in mind that there were, for example, guns branded "Acme" made by a different manufacturer at a later date than the "Acme" in this list. Since the history of guns made by such famous American manfacturers as Winchester, Remington, Parker, etc., has been gone into extensively by other authors, we have given them only brief mention.

Foreign guns are listed only when in common use by American shooters. Many imported guns, especially those by smaller makers of England were sold here but not in sufficient quantity to deserve comment.

Actual dates of manufacture, when known, have been stated. Those followed by a question mark are hazarded simply as an educated guess until authentic dates are known.

Although muzzle-loading guns were popular and enjoyed a share of the low-priced market during the period in question, they are not mentioned here. All guns listed are *breech-loading double-barrels* unless otherwise noted.

Company names are listed in CAPITAL LETTERS, gun names in *italics*.

F. J. Abbey   (See *Fred J. Abbey Co.*)

ABBEY, FRED J. CO.
43 S. Clark Street
Chicago, Ill.

Made guns under patents of George Abbey from 1874–77 in prices ranging from $40 to $200. They were underlever break action, hammer guns, including a heavy duck gun weighing twelve and a half pounds in 12-gauge. Also imported actions and barrels from both England and Belgium to be fit and finished under the Abbey name. The name was sold to Foss Bros. & Co., same address, in 1878. Foss then marketed the F. J. Abbey guns under the brand name of *Abbey & Foster*.

Abbey & Foster   (*See Fred J. Abbey Co.*)

Acme   Single barrel. Made by Davenport Arms Co. Sold by several mail-order houses in $8 price range.

The Acme   Hammer gun sold by Henry C. Squires, New York, for $65 in 1883.

Acme Arms Co.   Hammer gun, twist barrels. Sold by Cornwall & Jespersen, New York, for $17.75 in 1899.

N. R. Adams   Made N. R. Davis and their successors, Davis-Warner from 1908 to about 1917.

Aetna   (See *Harrington & Richardson*)

Alaska   (See *Hood Firearms Co.*)

Alexis   (See *Hood Firearms Co.*)

Allen   (See *Hopkins & Allen*)

ALLEN, ETHAN & Co.
Worcester, Mass.
Period 1868. Single barrel. Early U. S. breechloader using the Allen trap-door breech.

America   Hammer gun brand of Bliss & Goodyear (distributor), New Haven, Conn. Cheaply made, Belgian proofs.

AMERICAN ARMS CO.
103 Milk Street
Boston, Mass.
Started in 1861 making quality muzzle-loading double-barrels and pistols. Business was discontinued about 1875 and started anew in 1877. In 1881 the company offered a "swing-out" breech-loading hammer double-barrel that was a patent of George H. Fox. The gun was called "Fox," not to be confused with the A. H. Fox gun of later manufacture. The Fox 12-gauge with damascus barrels sold at $50 at the time of its introduction. It was reported well thought of and a quality gun in every respect. But the "swing-out" principle of ejection and loading did not find favor and the gun was discontinued around 1885. Although highly advertised in trade journals, it is thought that something less than 1,000 were ever produced. Ads of the late 80's stated there were only a few of the Fox guns left to be sold at reduced prices. While maintaining their Boston office, the factory was reportedly moved from Chicopee Falls, Mass. to Milwaukee, Wisc. in 1893. Sometime in 1899 it was moved to Bluffton, Ala. and started manufacture of another G. H. Fox patent, a hammerless double-barrel named "Whitmore." But some are known to be marked "Whittmore." These guns were sold through various outlets,

including Montgomery Ward's Chicago store. All assets were purchased by Marlin Firearms Co. in 1901 and machinery moved to New London, Conn.

American Barlock Wonder Sears Roebuck brand of hammer gun selling for $10.95 in their 1902 catalog.
American Boy Brand name of both single and double-barrel guns distributed by Townley Metal & Hardware Co., Kansas City, Mo.

American Field (See *Wm. P. Scott*)

American Gun Co. (See *H & D Folsom*)
American Hammerless Sold in 1883 by Clark & Sneider, 214 Pratt Street, Baltimore, Md. A side-lock gun with adjustable main spring. Made in 4, 8, 10, 12, and 20-gauge.

American Nitro American made single-barrel hammer gun. Nothing further known.

AMIET, AUGUST
Koch, Ohio
High quality single-barrel. Made from 1883–86.

Anson Hammerless Gun Made by FN of Belgium for European sales but appearing here in some quantity during the 90's.

Wm. Arden Six and a quarter pound 16-gauge with rebounding hammers. Sold for $40 in 1881 by Henry C. Squires, New York.

Aristocrat Brand of Supplee-Biddle Hardware Co., Philadelphia, Pa. Maker unknown.

Armstrong (See *G & A Hayden*)

ASSONET GUN FACTORY
Assonet, Mass.
1893–94. Made double-barreled guns. Nothing further known.

A. J. Aubrey Made by Meriden Firearms Co. Sold by Sears Roebuck about 1906. Different models ranging in price from $13.85 to $26.75.

BACON ARMS CO.
Norwich, Conn.
About 1875–90. Makers of pistols and revolvers, but reportedly made some double-barrels. All guns examined that were so marked have proven to be Belgian made and imported by H & D Folsom. (See next listing.)
Bacon Arms Co. (See *H & D Folsom*)

BAKER GUN & FORGING CO.
Batavia, N.Y.

Baker started in 1885 in Syracuse, New York, and was known as Syracuse Forging Co. The firm was moved to Batavia following a fire in 1889. First Bakers made in the Syracuse plant were hammer guns of 10 and 12-gauge with twist barrels and were known as the "Syracuse Model." Production was stopped on this gun in 1888 and a new design was offered — this a sidelock double. This gun was discontinued in 1896 after some 30,000 had been sold. It was followed by the new Baker hammer Model 1897, offered in two grades of 10, 12, and 16-gauge and priced from $25. A hammerless model was offered starting in the early 90's in grades A and B with prices of $35 and $50. In 1894 the Paragon grade was introduced at $60. Also made three-barrel gun 1881–87 in $125 grade.

Baker Gun Co. (See *H & D Folsom*)

BALDWIN & CO., LTD.
New Orleans, La.

Made 12-gauge hammer gun with octagonal barrels. Also imported a Belgian-made hammer gun called the "Sheffield."

BALTIMORE ARMS CO.
Baltimore, Md.

Made 12 Ga. hammerless from about 1895–1902.

T. Barker Also *Thomas Barker*. Sold by Sears Roebuck. (See *H & D Folsom*)

Bartlett Field Brand name of Hibbard, Spencer, Bartlett & Co., Chicago, Ill. English-made hammer gun selling in 1884 for $60 in 12 Ga., $65 in 10-gauge.

BAY STATE ARMS CO.
Uxbridge, Mass.

Started in Worcester, Mass. in 1870. Apparently discontinued in 1874. Reorganized business in 1880 and made "Bay State Gun." Later purchased by Hopkins & Allen who continued to make "Bay State" single barrel guns.

BECK, SAMUEL
Indianapolis, Ind.

Made high quality hammer guns to order, selling at $100 in 1879.

Belknap Brand name of Belknap Hardware Co.

Bellmore Gun Co. (See *H & D Folsom*)

Berkshire 12 gauge hammerless sold by Shapleigh Hardware Co., of St. Louis.

Big All Right 8-gauge hammer gun made by Wright Arms Co., Lawrence, Mass. in late 70's.

Black Beauty Brand name for Sears Roebuck. Belgian made hammer gun sold around 1900 for $11.25.

BLICKENSDOEFER & SCHILLING
12 S. Third Street
St. Louis, Mo.

1873–74. Primarily known for Schuetzen rifles. This firm also made a few high grade hammer guns with laminated steel barrels, excellent wood and engraving.

Blissard Side-lever hammer gun with steel barrels. Sold by Henry C. Squires, New York, for $50 in 1878.

Bogardus Club Gun Sold in 1887. Nothing further known.

C. G. Bonehill English-made gun of good repute. First offered in America in 1878 by Homer Fisher Co., 260 Broadway, New York. Later imported and sold by Charles J. Godfrey, New York, for $85 in 1881. Godfrey also sold a Bonehill-made gun called the "Complete Gun" for $40 in 1883. (Also see *H & D Folsom*)

Daniel Boone Brand name of Belknap Hardware Co., Louisville, Ky. Used on several models.

Boyd & Tyler Probably made by Boyd Breechloading Arms Co., 81 Washington St., Boston, Mass., in 1870–72. Said by some authorities to be first American breech-loading double-barrel produced in commercial quantities.

Bridge Gun Works Brand name of Shapleigh Hardware Co., St. Louis. Belgian made.

Bridgeport Arms Co. Belgian-made hammer gun. Brand name of Fred Biffar & Co., Chicago, Ill. Importer unknown.
Brooks (See *Brooks Arms & Tool Co.*)

BROOKS, C. C. ARMS & TOOL CO.
Portland, Me.
Made double barrels along with rifles and knives from 1888–1903.

James Brown & Son (See *Enterprise Gun Works*)
BROWN, R. H. & CO.
New Haven, Conn.
Primarily tool makers. Reportedly produced double-barrels from 1883–1904.

Saml. Buckley & Co. Hammer gun sold by J. Palmer O'Neil Co., Pittsburgh, Penn., 1880's.

Burdick Hammer gun with Damascus finish. Sold Sears Roebuck about 1905 for $8.65. Belgian proofs.

BURGESS GUN CO.
Buffalo, N.Y.

1893–99. Unusual pump-action shotgun, the invention of Andrew Burgess. The pistol grip along with trigger and trigger guard was moved to the rear to open action and eject fired shell, shoving pistol grip forward, loaded the gun, and locked breech. It was also made in a hinged take-down model, as well as riot gun with 20-inch barrel. Offered in choice of fluid steel at $30 or Damascus twist barrels at $40. The firm was bought by Winchester in 1899.

BUTLER, JOSEPH & CO.
179 E. Madison Street
Chicago, Ill.

About 1870–80. Primarily re-barrelers and choke borers, but made a few guns on W. & C. Scott actions carrying their own name.

Carolina Arms Co. (See *H & D Folsom*)

Central Arms Co. (See *H & D Folsom*)

Champion English made hammer gun sold by Henry C. Squires, New York, for $35 in 1877.

Champion Hammer single barrel sold in 1883 by John P. Lovell & Son, Boston, in grades $10 to $15. The name later used on single barrel guns by Iver Johnson.

Cherokee Arms Co. (See *H & D Folsom*)

Chesapeake Gun Co. (See *H & D Folsom*)

Chicago Brand name of Hibbard, Spencer, Bartlett Co., Hdw., Chicago, Ill. This name used on several different guns from late 80's into 1900's.

Chicago Long Range Wonder Hammerless gun sold by Sears Roebuck in 1902 for $15.95. Looks to be Crescent made. (See *H & D Folsom*)

J. P. Clabrough English made hammerless selling for $45 in 1900 by Schoverling, Daly & Gales, New York. Both fluid steel and Damascus were offered, as well as other models.

Clark & Sneider (See *C. W. Sneider*)

COLT PATENT FIREARMS MANUFACTURING CO.
Hartford, Conn.

Double-barrel hammer guns in 1878 and hammerless in 1883. Also a revolving shotgun.

COLTON FIREARMS CO.
Toledo, Ohio

Made hammer and hammerless, seemingly for Sears Roebuck only

Columbia Hammer with English twist barrels. Sold for $45 in 1883 by Henry C. Squires, New York.

COLUMBIAN FIREARMS CO.
Philadelphia, Penn.

No records. Said to have produced double-barreled guns, but more likely a brand name.

COLVIN, M. S.
Salamanka, N.Y.

Handmade hammerless of excellent quality, selling for $125 in 1882.

Compeer (See *H & D Folsom*)

Competition About late 80's brand name of John Meunier Gun Co., Water Street, Milwaukee, Wisc.

Continental (See *Great Western Gun Works*)

Crancers Field Gun Hammer with steel barrels. No proof marks, nothing further known.

CRESCENT FIREARMS CO.
Meriden, Conn.

(See *H & D Folsom*)

Creve Coeur Hammer Damascus. Belgian proofs. Thought to be brand name of Isaac Walker Hardware Co., Peoria, Ill.

Cruso (See *H & D Folsom*)

Cumberland Arms Co. (See *H & D Folsom*)

Charles Daly Excellent guns — hammer, hammerless, and 3-barrel. A house brand of Schoverling, Daly and Gales, 84 Chambers Street, New York. The Daly brand was first made by Lindner of Prussia and later by J. P. Sauer of Germany. These guns sold from $95 to $325 for the diamond grade in 1900. The three-barrel gun, a hammer model, was offered in 10 and 12-guage with rifle calibers of 32 W.C.F., 32/40, 38/55, 40/63, and 45/70.

DANE, J. C.
LaCrosse, Wisc.

Good quality hammer gun selling for $85 in 1877 and marked "Dane." Marketed by Camp & Wise, Stoughton, Wisc.

DAVENPORT, W. H. FIREARMS CO.
Started 1880 at 79 Orange Street, Providence, R.I. Quit business about 1883 and reorganized in 1890 at Norwich, Conn. Known mostly for top-break, single-barrel shotguns, but also made a lever action with sliding breech lock. Also made guns marked "Keystone Firearms Co., Phila, Pa." A private brand name of the E. K. Tryon Co. Made cheap single-barrels under many private brand names for wholesale hardware firms.

Davis   Hammer Damascus, no proofs. Possibly N. R. Davis.

DAVIS, N. R. & CO.
Assonet, Freetown, Me.

1883. Made hammer and a good quality hammerless selling for $65 in 1887 and marked "Rival." Also made guns under Sears Roebuck brand names. Later Davis-Warner Arms Co.

Delphian   12 gauge hammer with known serial numbers up to 371972 and marked elsewhere on gun "Delphian Manufacturing Co." No proofs. Not believed connected with Delphian Arms Co. Possibly Crescent made. (See *H & D Folsom*)

Delphian Arms Co.   Brand name for Supplee-Biddle Hdw. Co., Philadelphia, Pa.

Demon   English made by Midland Gun Co. and quite common here in the late 90's.

DETROIT ARMS CO.
Detroit, Mich.

Said to have made double-barrels. Nothing further known.

Diamond Arms Co.   Brand name of Shapleigh Hdw. Co., St. Louis, Mo.

Amos Dickerman   Hammerless single-barrel made in 1881 by Strong Firearms Co., New Haven, Conn. Later made to 1888 by Amos Dickerman, New Haven, Conn.

DODDS, JAMES
Dayton, Ohio

1866–91. Made both breech- and muzzle-loading guns to order.

DONN, JAMES & BRO.
Canton, Ill.

1880–84. This firm made hammer guns under the "Donn" brand and advertised in 1883 they had, "secured the services of skilled workmen direct from the leading gun manufactories of London, Manchester, and Birmingham, and are now prepared to turn out work that cannot be excelled either in quality, style, durability, or finish with the twenty-five years' experience of James Donn in the manufacture of fine guns". They were also importers, distributors, and assemblers, all under the brand name "Donn."

Dougall English made. Their "lock-fast" hammerless with choked barrels sold in their "best" grade for $450 in 1887. Their pigeon model, a 12-gauge weighing six and three-quarters pounds, was popular among the live-bird shooters.

Dunlap Special Brand name of Dunlap Hdw. Co., Macon, Ga., and used on guns from both Davis-Warner and H & D Folsom.

Eastern Arms Co. J. Stevens brand. Probably starting about 1910–15.

Eclipse Belgian made. Sold by E. C. Meacham Arms Co., St. Louis, Mo.

Elgin Arms Co. (See *H & D Folsom*)

Elita Single barrel made by Davenport Arms Co.
Richard Ellis English made. Their circular hammer and hammerless guns were quite popular in the early 1880's.

ELMIRA ARMS CO.
Elmira, N.Y.

A distributor marketing guns under its own name and the brand name "Queen City." (Also see *H & D Falsom*)

Empire (See *H & D Folsom*)

Empire Arms Co. Sears Roebuck brand name. (See *H & D Folsom*)

Enders Oak Leaf and *Enders Royal Service* (See *H & D Folsom*)

ENTERPRISE GUN WORKS
136 Wood Street
Pittsburgh, Pa.

Owned by James Brown & Sons, 1871–82. Made several models medium grade hammer guns. Also imported under their name.

Essex (See *H & D Folsom*)

Wm. Evans William Evans was formerly with Purdey & Sons. In the late 80's made 10 and 12-gauge hammer and hammerless for the American market. Fine quality guns with prices between $200 and $400. The firm still exists in London.

Excel   Montgomery Ward brand. Double-barrel maker unknown; single-barrel maker was Iver Johnson.

Farwell Arms Co.   Brand name of Farwell, Ozmun, Kirk & Co., St. Paul, Minn.
Faultless and *Faultless Goose Gun*   (See *H & D Folsom*)

The Featherlight   Sears Roebuck brand.

The Field   (See *H & D Folsom*)

512 Gun   Hammer Damascus. Sold for $25 with case and loading tools in 1887. Offered by White & Wills, 232 State Street, Chicago.

H & D FOLSOM ARMS CO.
312-14 Broadway
New York, N.Y.

The history of H & D Folsom is a foggy field. The company stated they had been in business since 1859, but apparently they measured from the time Henry Folsom was a gunsmith. Several changes in style and name of doing business were made throughout the years. For the purpose of this book, the company may be picked up in 1890 as an importer and distributor of firearms and general sporting goods.

Some three years later, Folsom purchased the Crescent Fire Arms Co., of Norwich, Conn., makers of single and double barrel shotguns. The original Crescent model guns were sold until about 1895 when two new models appeared with design attributed to Frank A. Foster. At this time, new and more modern machinery was purchased and guns retailed directly by Folsom's brand name, American Gun Co. The same guns were offered under house brands of hardware wholesalers and sporting goods firms throughout the country.

As of 1897 they were made in five grades. Factory #2641 was a top lever action double-barrel with armory steel barrels, double bolt, and of barlock with low circular hammers. It was made in 12-gauge only with thirty inch or thirty-two inch barrels and sold under the American Arms Co. brand at $14.

Factory # 2650 was essentially the same gun in a better finished model with damascus barrels and retailing at $15. Both of the above guns used Belgian made barrels.

Factory #2660 was American made throughout and of same general design but carried American made damascus barrels, selling at $18.

Factory #2655 of same design but with twist barrels and a Deeley & Edge snap fore-end, plus engraving on locks and trigger guard. Sold also at $18.

Factory #2665 was also same design, differing only in greater coverage of engraving and sold for $20. Hammerless models followed, but were still based on the original Foster design.

Folsom, at one and the same time, was importing English, French, and Belgian guns, all in low and medium price range, and taking contracts to furnish either their own or imported guns under any brand name the purchaser desired.

This type of operation was continued until 1930 when a merger was made with Davis-Warner Arms Corp., which became the Crescent-Davis Arms Corp. Its machinery and assets were bought two years later by Stevens Arms Co., but the name H & D Folsom Arms Co. was continued at the same New York address where they became retailers and jobbers. In 1954 the company was sold to Universal Tackle & Sporting Goods Co., also of New York, who then assumed the Folsom name and continue today in Yonkers, N.Y. and Tampa, Fla. as distributors. According to present owners, company records were either lost or destroyed during several moves, and no longer exist.

The following listing of Crescent-made and Folsom-imported guns is thought to be far from complete but should assist in clearing much of the confusion that exists in identifying the maker or importer and distributor of these various brand name guns. The actual dates these brands were first used are in most cases impossible to obtain. For this reason many names may lap into the World War I period and perhaps after. It should also be understood that many of these private brand names were used by the distributor owning the name on rifles and pistols, as well as shotguns of makers other than Folsom.

American Gun Co. Crescent made. Principal house brand of Folsom until acquisition of Baker Gun Co. Used for direct sales and to firms not wishing to use their own brand names. The hammer model sold by Sears in 1902 for $10.22. Hammerless models followed and usually carried additional marking on action of "Knickerbocker."

Bacon Arms Co. Usually hammer with Belgian proofs.

Baker Gun Co. Used on both Crescent and Belgian guns.

T. Barker Both Belgian and Crescent made for Sears Roebuck brand. Hammer guns in grades from $10.40 to $27.50.

Carolina Arms Co. Crescent for Smith-Wadsworth Hdw. Co., of Charlotte, N.C.

Central Arms Co. Crescent for Shapleigh Hdw. Co., St. Louis, Mo.

Cherokee Arms Co.   Crescent for C. M. McClung & Co., Knoxville, Tenn.

Chesapeake Gun Co.   Folsom house brand. Crescent made.

Compeer   Crescent for Van Camp Hdw. Co., Indianapolis, Ind.

Cruso   Crescent for Hibbard, Spencer, Bartlett Co., Chicago, Ill.

Cumberland Arms Co.   Crescent for Gray & Dudley Hdw. Co., Nashville, Tenn.

Elgin Arms Co.   Crescent for Fred Biffar & Co. and also Strauss & Schram, both Chicago, Ill.

Elmira Arms Co.   Crescent for Elmira Arms Co., Elmira, N.Y.

Empire   Crescent made; Folsom house brand.

Empire Arms Co.   Crescent for Sears.

Enders Oak Leaf and *Enders Royal Service*   Both Crescent for Shapleigh Hdw., St. Louis.

Essex   Crescent for Belknap Hdw. Co., Louisville, Ky.

Faultless   Crescent for John M. Smythe Co., Chicago, Ill.

The Field   Hammer single barrel, 10 and 12 Ga. Not actually a Folsom brand name but sold by them in 1883 from their retail store.

F. F. Forbes   Crescent; Folsom house brand.

C. W. Franklin   Belgian made; Folsom house brand.

Harrison Arms Co. (Frank)   Belgian for Sickles & Preston, Davenport, Ia.

Hartford Arms Co.   Crescent for Simmons Hdw. and Shapleight Hdw., both of St. Louis.

Harvard   Crescent; Folsom house brand.

Henry Gun Co.   Belgian; Folsom house brand.

Hermitage Arms Co. and *Hermitage Gun Co.*   Crescent for Gray & Dudley Hdw. Co., Nashville, Tenn.

Howard Arms Co.   Crescent for Fred Biffar Co., Chicago.

Hummer   Belgian for Lee Hdw. Co., Salina, Kans.

Interstate Arms Co.   Crescent for Townley Metal & Hdw. Co., Kansas City, Mo.

Jackson Arms Co.   Crescent for C. M. McClung Co., Knoxville, Tenn.

Kingsland Special and *Kingsland 10 Star*   Crescent for Geller, Ward & Hasner, St. Louis, Mo.

Knickerbocker   Crescent. Much used Folsom house brand.

Knox-All   Crescent and Iver Johnson. Folsom house brand.

Lakeside   Crescent for Montgomery Ward.

J. H. Lau & Co.   Crescent; name of distributor not known.

Leader Gun Co.   Crescent for Chas. Williams Stores, New York, N.Y.

Lee Special and *Lee's Munner Special*   Crescent for Lee Hdw. Co., Salina, Kans.

Liege Arms Co.   Belgian for Hibbard, Spencer, Bartlett. 10 and 12 Ga. selling for $45 in 1884. This among first private branding of imports done by Folsom.

J. Manton & Co.   Belgian; Folsom house brand.

Marshwood   For Chas. Williams Stores.

Massachusetts Arms Co.   For Bish, Mize & Stillman Hdw. Co., Atchison, Kans.

Metropolitan   Crescent for Siegel-Cooper Co., New York.

Minnesota Arms Co.   For Farwell, Ozmun & Kirk, St. Paul, Minn.

Mississippi Valley Arms Co.   Crescent for Shapleigh Hdw. Co., St. Louis.

Mohawk   For Bish, Mize & Stillman Hdw. Co., Atchison, Kans.

Monitor   For Paxton & Gallagher Co., Omaha, Neb.

Wm. Moore & Co.   The original Wm. Moore & Co. produced an English "Best" gun in side action. *Wm. Moore & Co.* was also used on Belgian barlocks by Folsom, selling in a hammer gun of 12 and 14 Ga. for $13.50 in 1884.

Mt. Vernon Arms Co.   Belgian; Folsom house brand.

National Arms Co.   Crescent; Folsom house brand in double-barrel. Do not confuse with "National Arms Co." branded pump gun made by Marlin.

New Rival   Crescent for Van Camp Hdw. Co., Indianapolis.

New York Arms Co.   Crescent for Garnet-Carter Co., Chattanooga, Tenn.

Nitro Bird   For Richards & Conover Hdw. Co., Kansas City, Mo.

Nitro Hunter   For Belknap Hdw. Co., Louisville.

Norwich Arms Co.   Crescent for Sears Roebuck. Hammer gun selling $11.72 and $13.22 in 1908.

Not-Nac Manufacturing Co.   Crescent for Belknap Hdw. Co., Louisville. Also for Canton Hdw. Co., Canton, Ohio.

Oxford Arms Co.   Crescent for Belknap Hdw. Co.

C. Parker & Co.   Belgian; Folsom house brand.

Peerless   Crescent; Folsom house brand.

Perfection   Crescent for H. G. Lipscomb & Co., Nashville, Tenn.

Piedmont   Crescent for Piedmont Hdw. Co., Danville, Penn.

Pioneer Arms Co.   Belgian for Kruse Hdw. Co., Cincinnati, Ohio.

Quail   Crescent; Folsom house brand.

Queen City   Crescent for Elmira Arms Co., Elmira, New York.

Rev-O-Noc   Crescent for Hibbard, Spencer, Bartlett Co., Chicago.

W. Richards   Belgian; Folsom house brand.

Richter (Charles)   Crescent for New York Sporting Goods Co., New York.

Rickard Arms Co.   Crescent for J. A. Rickard Co., Schenectady, N.Y.

Royal Service   For Shapleigh Hdw. Co., St. Louis.

Rummel   Crescent for A. J. Rummel Arms Co., Toledo, Ohio.

St. Louis Arms Co.   Belgian for both Shapleigh Hdw. and Sears Roebuck in 1897.

Shue's Special   For Ira M. Shue, Hanover, Penn.

Sickel's Arms Co.   Belgian for Robert Sickel & Preston Co., Davenport, Ia.

Southern Arms Co.   Crescent; distributor unknown.

Special Service   For Shapleigh Hdw.

Spencer Gun Co.   Crescent for Hibbard, Spencer, Bartlett, Chicago.

Sportsmen   Crescent for W. Bingham Co., Cleveland, Ohio.

Springfield Arms Co.   Crescent; Folsom house brand. This brand also used on Stevens and James Warner guns.

Square Deal   Crescent for Stratton-Warren Hdw., Memphis, Tenn.

Stanley   Belgian; Folsom house brand.

State Arms Co.   Crescent for J. H. Lau & Co., address unknown.

H. J. Sterling   Belgian; distributor unknown.

Sullivan Arms Co.   Crescent; distributor unknown.

Ten Star and *Ten Star Heavy Duty*   For Geller, Ward & Hasner, St. Louis.

Tiger   Belgian for J. H. Hall Co., Nashville, Tenn.

Triumph   One of several names used on guns made by Crescent under Charles Lancaster patents. All 12 Ga. hammerless, twist barrels. Sold by Sears Roebuck at $27.50 in 1897.

U. S. Arms Co.   Crescent for Supplee-Biddle Hdw. Co.

Victor and *Victor Special*   Crescent for Hibbard, Spencer, Bartlett, Chicago. Both single and double barrels.

Virginia Arms Co. Crescent for Virginia-Caroline Co., Richmond, Va.

Volunteer For Belknap Hdw.

Vulcan Arms Co. Crescent; Folsom house brand.

Warren Arms Co. Belgian; Folsom house brand.

Wilkinson Arms Co. Belgian for Richmond Hdw., Richmond, Va.

Wilmont Arms Co. Belgian; Folsom house brand.

Wilshire Arms Co. For Stauffer, Eshleman & Co., New Orleans, La.

Wiltshire Arms Co. Belgian; Folsom house brand.

Winfield Arms Co. Crescent; Folsom house brand.

Winoca Arms Co. Crescent for Jacobi Hdw., Co., Philadelphia, Penn.

Wolverine For Fletcher Hdw., Co., Wilmington, N.C.

Worthington Arms Co. Crescent for Geo. Worthington Co., Cleveland, Ohio.

In addition to the above guns there are Folsom "possibles". It has become commonplace for authorities to credit H & D Folsom for any vintage double barrel of unknown origin. The following list is of guns that look like, are thought to be, or have been claimed as imported or made by Folsom; but, as of yet, the relationship has not been definitely established.

Chicago Long Range Wonder Hammerless, sold by Sears Roebuck for $15.95 in 1902. Thought to have been supplied to Sears by both N. R. Davis and Crescent.

Delphian 12-gauge hammer gun. Also marked "Delphian Manufacturing Co."

Hanover Arms Co. Hammer, Damascus.

S. H. Harrington Hammer, Damascus. Belgian proofs.

Hunter Most likely Crescent made for Belknap Hdw. Co.

Long Range Wonder Sears Roebuck brand in both hammer and hammerless.

F. A. Loomis Hammer 12 Ga., laminated steel. No proofs.

Mears Hammer, Damascus.

Newport A brand name of Hibbard, Spencer, Bartlett, appearing on several guns, including some thought to be Crescent made.

New York Machine Made Hammer, laminated steel. Sold for $60 about 1890. Said to be a product of the original Crescent Arms Co.

Pagoma Thought to be Crescent, for Paxton, Gallagher Hdw. Co.

Paragon Hammer, Damascus.

Parkhurst   Belgian. Hammer, Damascus.

Pittsfield   Brand name Hibbard, Spencer, Bartlett.

Red Chieftain   Brand name Supplee-Biddle Hdw. Co.

Ruso   Brand name Hibbard, Spencer, Bartlett. Both single and double barrels. Some thought to be Crescent made.

Russell Arms Co.   Belgian. Hammer, Damascus.

Star Leader   Thought to be Crescent.

Syco   Double, hammerless. Brand name Wyeth Hardware Co., St. Joseph, Mo.

Traps Best   Brand name Watkins-Cottrell Co., Richmond, Va.

Wautauga   Brand name Wallace Hardware Co., Morristown, Tenn.

Whippet   Brand name Hibbard, Spencer, Bartlett.

While names were numerous, the author estimates there were no more than four basic models made by Crescent, and probably less than fifteen different designs from eight European makers. The Crescent guns may be divided roughly into two designs — hammer and hammerless. From there it was but a question of difference in finish, wood, engraving, checkering, barrel steel, etc.

No other company approaches H & D Folsom in sheer numbers of brand-named guns. Certainly the double barrel collector could spend a lifetime building his collection of these guns alone and never know if it were complete.

Fogerty   (See *George F. Fogerty*)

FOGERTY, GEORGE F.
Cambridge, Mass.
Patented double-barrel of good quality around 1892. This gun is quite rare and few are known to have been made.

FOLK'S GUN WORKS
Ohio
1885–89. Made double-barrel hammer guns. Nothing further known.

F. F. Forbes   (See *H & D Folsom*)

FOREHAND ARMS CO.
Worcester, Mass.
This company went under the name of Forehand & Wadsworth from 1872 until 1890 when it became the Forehand Arms Co. which produced both hammer and hammerless guns under their own name and brand names for Sears Roebuck. Their hammerless sold at $33 and hammer at $22.90, in

1893, with choices of Damascus or fluid steel barrels. Also made a single barrel marketed at $12, and the same gun for Sears which they offered at $6.90. This company was later bought by Hopkins & Allen.

James H. Foster   Top break double-barrel made to order in 1879 and sold by E. Thomas, 186 Clark Street, Chicago. Was connected with Abbey & Foster Co. See Fred J. Abbey Co.

Fox   (See *American Arms Co.*)

FOX, A. H., GUN CO.
Philadelphia, Pa.

Ansley H. Fox, of Baltimore, was an exception among famous American gun designers in that he was a champion live bird shooter. Whether the first "A. H. Fox" double-barrel was made in Boston, Baltimore, or Philadelphia is a question mark. The gun appeared in the hands of shooters in the early 1880's and there is little mention of it in print at that time. All guns were of boxlock construction. There were many grades, and good examples are much sought after today. The brand name was later taken over by Savage.

C. W. Franklin   (See *H & D Folsom*)

Fyrberg & Co. (Andrew)   Brand name of Sears Roebuck.

Gallagher   Single-barrel made by Richardson & Overman, of Philadelphia, from 1868 to 1874.

GARDNER GUN CO.
80 Bank Street
Cleveland, Ohio
1887–95. Made good grade hammerless. Production small.

Gibralter   Brand name of Sears Roebuck.

Gladiator   Brand name of Sears Roebuck.

GODFREY, CHARLES J.
7 Warren Street
New York, N.Y.

Importers and dealers. Sold many guns by Enos James, Bonehill, and others. Their house brand "Knickerbocker Club Gun" was made for them by Enos James and sold in large quantity during mid-1880's. It was a hammer gun offered in $50 and $75 grades, in 10 and 12-gauge. The firm also sold a Bonehill-made gun under the "Chas. J. Godfrey" brand for $40, and were the distributors for I Hollis & Sons guns which they avertised in 1883 in the following grades: "Complete Gun", 40; "Prize Trap", $45; "Prize Field", $70, the latter gun being offered in 10, 12, and 16 gauges.

GREAT WESTERN GUN WORKS
285 Liberty Street
Pittsburgh, Pa.

Owned by J. H. Johnson who started business in 1865 making single-barrel breechloaders from old Springfield barrels. By 1888 the firm was offering imported double-barrels under brand name "Continental" in two styles, both hammer guns, a back action selling at $20 and a sidelock at $24. Their motto was, "Cheap guns for the people."

GREEN & ALLING
3 W. Main Street
Rochester, N.Y.

Actually manufactured muzzleloaders. All breechloaders bearing the "Green & Alling" name were by C. H. Green. (See *Charles H. Green*)

Charles H. Green Hammer, Damascus. Built on C. H. Green patents and imported by Green & Alling 1871–79.
E. C. Green This is the English made Edwinson C. Green which in 1883 was first and exclusivley imported by G & A Hayden, Jacksonville, Ill. It was a very well made and extremely popular pigeon gun having once won the London Field's Gun Trial over Greener. (See *G & A Hayden*)

GREENER, W. W., LTD.
St. Mary's Row
Birmingham, England

Guns marked "W.W." were made between 1860–79. This was probably the most famous of all English guns in America. Their American agency was Henry C. Squires, 1 Cortland Street, New York, N.Y.

Greenfield Brand name of Hibbard, Spencer, Bartlett Co.

H.S.B. & Co. (See *Hibbard, Spencer, Bartlett Co.*)

HACKETT, EDWIN
104 William Street
New York, N.Y.

Made high quality hammer gun about 1877. Edwin Hackett was formerly with Hackett Bros., of England. His guns were known for close and even patterning.

Hanover Arms Co. Hammer gun of unknown origin. (See *H & D Folsom*)

Hanscomb Brand name of Hanscomb Hdw. Co., Haverhill, Md.

HARRINGTON & RICHARDSON
Worcester, Mass.

1888 to date. Their early guns were hammerless, made on the Anson & Deeley patent, selling in the 1890's No. 1 grade, $100; No. 2 grade, $150; No. 3 grade, $200; No. 4 grade, $300. The gun was widely sold by Schoverling, Daly & Gales, wholesale distributors. There are reports of a gun being marked only "Automatic Hammerless" and known to be of H & R manufacture.

S. H. Harrington   (See *H & D Folsom*)

Harrison Arms Co. (Frank)   (See *H & D Folsom*)

Hartford Arms Co.   (See *H & D Folsom*)

HARTLEY & GRAHAM
17 Maiden Lane
New York, N.Y.

Known to have distributed guns marked with their name in 1874.

Harvard   (See *H & D Folsom*)

HASDELL, T. R.
70 E. Madison Street
Chicago, Ill.

Gunsmiths and dealers who in the early 80's made both hammer and hammerless guns under their own name. Most were made to order in a price range of $150 to $350. All known models were made from English action and barrels, with the higher priced models from W. & C. Scott & Sons. The firm also did rebarreling and was noted for their choke boring that produced extra tight patterns. They were renowned among live bird shooters.

HAYDEN, G & A
Jacksonville, Ill.

Imported *E. C. Green* and *Armstrong* hammer guns in the early 80's.

Henry Gun Co.   (See *H & D Folsom*)
Hercules   Brand name of both Montgomery Ward and Iver Johnson.

Hermitage Arms Co. and *Hermitage Gun Co.*   (See *H & D Folsom*)

Hexagon   Sears Roebuck brand selling for $12.35 in 1908.

Hib Spe Bar   Brand name Hibbard, Spencer, Bartlett Co.

Hibbard   Brand name Hibbard, Spencer, Bartlett Co.

HIBBARD, SPENCER, BARTLETT & CO.
Lake Street & Wabash Avenue
Chicago, Ill.

This firm quite active from 1880 as importers and distributors. A large wholesale hardware firm maintaining a complete gunsmithing and repair shop, as well as extensive gun sales department. Marketed guns under many of their own brand names.

Hollenbeck   (See *Hollenbeck Gun Co.*)

HOLLENBECK GUN CO.
18th & Chapline Streets
Wheeling, W. V.

1901. In 1903 moved to Moundsville, W.V. Frank Hollenbeck was connected with Syracuse Arms Co., who manufactured under Hollenbeck patents. The Hollenbeck Gun Co. made a three-barrel gun in several gauges and calibers, most popular being 12-gauge/.32-40 which sold for around $150 at the turn of the century. These guns are marked "Three-Barrel Gun Co., Wheeling, W.V.". Some models are marked "Royal Gun Co. and were made in the name factory, bearing the same patent mark, "Patd. Feb. 13, 1900." Total production was less than 2,000. Apparently double-barrel shotguns were made under all three names, "Hollenbeck Gun Co," "Three-Barrel Gun Co.," and "Royal Gun Co." There was also a single barrel trap gun made in limited numbers and known to be marked "Royal Gun Co." and "Hollenbeck Gun Co." The firm ceased production about 1910. All were hammerless box lock. Also see Syracuse Arms Co.

I. Hollis & Sons   (See *Charles J. Godfrey*)

Sam Holt   (See *S. Holt Arms Co.*)

S. Holt Arms Co.   Sears Roebuck brand name on Belgian hammer gun, "Raleigh steel" barrels. Sold in 1902 for $9.40.

HOOD FIREARMS CO.
Norwich, Conn.

1875–77. Known for revolvers, but either made or marketed double barrels under the brand names "Alexis" and "Alaska."

HOPKINS & ALLEN
Norwich, Conn.

Started producing arms in 1868. By 1886 were making single barrel guns in steel at $9, and Stubbs twist steel at $10. Also a lever action single barrel at $8.

Howard Arms Co.   (See *H & D Folsom*, also *Whitney Arms Co.*)

Hudson   Brand name Hibbard, Spencer, Bartlett Co.

Hummer   (See *H & D Folsom*)˙

Hunter   (See *H & D Folsom*)

HUNTER ARMS CO.
Fulton, N.Y.
(See *L. C. Smith Gun Co.*)

Illinois Arms Co.   Sears Roebuck brand name for a pump gun they offered for $15.96 in 1906.

Infallible   Brand name of Davis-Warner Arms Co. about 1917. (See *N. R. Davis*)

Interchangeable   Belgian hammer gun; also marked "Occidental". Nothing further known.

International   Brand name for Meacham Arms Co., St. Louis, Mo.

Interstate Arms Co.   (See *H & D Folsom*)

ITHACA GUN CO.
Ithaca, N.Y.
1873 to date. During the years, Ithaca absorbed the Union Firearms Co., Syracuse Arms Co., Wilkesbarre Gun Co., and Lefever Arms Co. Ithaca started manufacture of guns in 1880, the first being a hammer model of Baker design and which continued until 1893 when they produced a hammerless model with design attributed to Fred Crass. All were box lock actions and barreled in damascus or twist steel only until after the turn of the century. The Ithaca policy was always quality guns at reasonable prices. Shortly after the turn of the century, hammerless guns were offered in grades No. 1½ at $31.50; No. 2D at $42.75; No. 2K at $49.87; No. 3 at $60, and No. 4 at $75. Barreling at this time was done in Damascus or Krupp fluid steel. Shortly thereafter, Ithaca increased their offerings to eighteen grades, and by 1915 had introduced their famous single barrel trap gun.

Jackson Arms Co.   (See *H & D Folsom*)

Enos James   (See *Charles J. Godfrey*)

JOHNSON, IVER, ARMS & CYCLE WORKS
Fitchburg, Mass.
1871 to date. Iver Johnson shotgun production began in 1891 in Fitchburg, Mass., making both single and double barrels. Around 1900 the firm produced

a great many single barrel guns under various brand names for hardware and mailorder firms — all of low and medium price.

J. H. Johnson   (See *Great Western Gun Works*)

LOUIS JORDAN
71 and 73 East Randolph Street
Chicago, Ill.
Awarded metal at Columbian Exposition, 1893.

M.F. KENNEDY & BROS.
134 East Third Street
St. Paul, Minn.
Advertisements read "Established 1867. Manufacturers of fine breech-loading shotguns."

Keystone   (See *Davenport Arms Co.*)

King-Nitro   Brand name Shapleigh Hdw. Co., St. Louis.

Kingsland Special   (See *H & D Folsom*)

Kingsland 10 Star   (See *H & D Folsom*)

Kirk Gun Co.   Brand name Farwell, Ozmun & Kirk, St. Paul, Minn.

KIRKWOOD, D.
24 Elm Street
Boston, Mass.
Known as Mortimer & Kirkwood until 1879. In 1883 made hammerless three-barrel gun and hammerless double barrel in $100, $150, and $200 grades. They also made a specialty of altering regular double barrels to three-barrel guns.

KITTREDGE, B., & CO.
Cincinnati, Ohio
Sold Belgian-made guns under their name in 1881.

Knickerbocker   (See *H & D Folsom*)

Knickerbocker Club Gun   (See *Charles J. Godfrey*)

Knox-All   (See *H & D Folsom*) Guns marked with this private brand were also made by Iver Johnson.

G. Lafley   High grade hammer, Damascus. Sold by H. C. Squires for $275 in 1878.

Lakeside   Montgomery Ward brand name. (See *H & D Folsom*)

Chas. Lancaster   High grade English guns in many models. Much in use here. Made a pigeon gun especially for the American market in 1887. It was priced at $150, carried laminated steel barrels, chambered for a two and three-quarters inch shell, rebounding back-action locks, with hammers below line of sight.

J. H. Lau & Co.   (See *H & D Folsom*)

Leader Gun Co.   (See *H & D Folsom*)

Lee Special and *Lee's Munner Special*   (See *H & D Folsom*)

W. R. Leeson   Good grade, English made. Screw grip action in hammer and hammerless. Their advertising in 1883 asked the reader to "Place your order direct," and guns were listed from $128 to $198, plus duty.

LEFEVER ARMS CO.
213 Malthrie Street
Syracuse, N.Y.
1892–1908. (See *D. M. Lefever Sons & Co.*)

LEFEVER, D. M., SONS & CO.
Syracuse, N.Y.
Daniel M. Lefever started as a small gunsmith of Auburn, N.Y. around 1853. Four years later found him operating in Canandaigua, N.Y., and by 1863 he had moved to a partnership in Syracuse, N.Y. that was to produce "Lefever & Ellis" guns. In 1876 he entered into another partnership with John A. Nichols which resulted in the then famous "Nichols & Lefever" guns. John Nichols had formerly made some of the finest breechloading shotguns in the country. They incorporated Nichols' 1877 patent on a thumb operated release of the breech, and used English made Damascus barrels. The Nichols-Lefever partnership was to last but a short time, with Nichols purchasing the name as well as the gunmaking machinery of L. Barber & Co. to make and market the gun on his own.

   Dan Lefever opened his own business again in 1879 at 78 N. Water Street, in Syracuse, where he made hammerless side-break guns to order, as well as three-barrel guns, until selling part of his patents and his name to another concern which used the name "Lefever Arms Co."

   In 1902 he again went into business for himself as D. M. Lefever Sons & Co., 207 N. Franklin Street, Syracuse, and made a specialty of featherweight double-barrels in 16 and 20 guage, weighing as little as five pounds. At this time his advertising always contained the phrase, "Not connected with Lefever Arms Co."

   During his time in business Lefever produced many hammer guns, as well as one of the first U. S. made hammerless in 1878. They were in gauges 8,

10, 12, 16, and 20, with tapered choke guaranteed to pattern seventy-five per cent in full.

Early Lefever guns were a rarity in being U. S.-made sidelocks. Lefever often fought claims his design was a sidelock modification of Westley Richards' boxlock and denied this by pointing out that the Westley Richards rib extension was in doll's head form, which he asserted was a wedge tending to spread the breech. The "Lefever" gun was made with a square shouldered extension.

The Ithaca Gun Co. purchased the "Lefever" gun in 1915 and continued to use the name on boxlock guns. "Lefevers" serial numbered over 100,000 were Ithaca-made.

G. E. Lewis & Sons This Birmingham made gun was imported by the V.L. & D. Co., of New York, in 1874, the most famous model being their long-range duck gun. While some guns sold as low as $75, there was the "Guarantee" model at $150, and the "Excelsior" at $200.

Liège Arms Co. (See *H & D Folsom*)

Long-Range Wonder Sears Roebuck brand name of about 1899 appearing on both hammer and hammerless. (Also see *H. & D. Folsom*)

Long Tom Sears Roebuck brand name for single-barrel as long as thirty-six inches, and appearing on many models over a lengthy period.

F. A. Loomis Hammer 12-gauge, laminated barrels. No proof marks. Nothing further known.

LOVELL, JOHN P., ARMS CO.
145 Washington Street
Boston, Mass.

Started in 1879 and by 1890 had moved to 147 Wade Street, at which time the firm was sold to Charles J. Godfrey Co. Lovell was best known for its "Champion" and "Top-Snap" single-barrels selling in the $10 range. They also marketed a 10-gauge double-barrel called "Favorite" selling at $75, but it is not known whether Lovell actually made this gun or imported it for sale.

Mahillon (Emile) Belgian-made hammer gun of top grade selling for $200 in 1898. Importer unknown.

Manhattan Arms Co. Brand name of Schoverling, Daly, & Gales, of New York; sold in both hammer and hammerless during late 1880's.

J. Manton & Co. (See *H & D Folsom*)

MARLIN FIREARMS CO.
New Haven, Conn.

Model 1898 hammer pump gun in 12-gauge. List price in early 1900's was $22.50.

Marshwood (See *H & D Folsom*)

Saml. Marson & Co. English made hammer double-barrel. Importer unknown.

Massachusetts Arms Co. (See *H & D Folsom*)

MEACHAM, E. C., ARMS CO. (Also C. D.)
St. Louis, Mo.

1880–92. Sold hammerless, Damascus marked "E. C. Mac, St. Louis." 10 and 12-gauge, $36 in 1891. Perhaps made or imported other models.

Mears (See *H & D Folsom*)

MERIDEN FIRE ARMS CO.
Meriden, Conn.

A subsidiary of Sears Roebuck & Co., actually manufacturing guns for sale exclusively by the parent company. They also imported guns from Germany and Belgium under their name. Sears sold the factory for $50,000 to Westinghouse Electric & Manufacturing Co., in 1915, and the factory appears not to have made guns again.

Metropolitan (See *H & D Folsom*)

Edward Middleton A bottom break, back-action, hammer gun with laminated steel barrels. Nothing further known.

Midland Gun Co. English made at Demon Gun Works, of Birmingham.

Minnesota Arms Co. (See *H & D Folsom*)

Mississippi Valley Arms Co. (See *H & D Folsom*)

Mohawk (See *H & D Folsom*)

Monitor (See *H & D Folsom*)

Wm. Moore & Co. Good grade English gun in side-action. (For barlock, see *H & D Folsom*.)

Chas. Mortimer Believed formerly associated with Mortimer & Kirkwood, Boston, Mass., and going into business for himself when that firm closed in 1880. Known to have made a 16-gauge Damascus, hammer gun selling with a trunk case for $75 in 1881.

Mt. Vernon Arms Co.   (See *H & D Folsom*)

Mullen (Patrick)   Seemingly short-lived, the Mullen gun was well spoken of in 1887. Known to have made an 8-gauge weighing 18 pounds with forty-inch barrels, and a 12 pound 10-gauge with thirty-six inch barrels.

National Arms Co.   Pump gun made by Marlin. (For double-barrel, see *H & D Folsom.*)

New Aubrey   Sears Roebuck brand name.

New England Arms Co.   Brand name of Charles J. Godfrey, used on Belgian import.

New Era Gun Works   Hammerless, damascus barreled. No proofs. Patent marks Aug. 12, 1884. Also marked on action "New York Nitro Hammerless." Nothing further known.

Newport   (See *H & D Folsom*)

New Rival   (See *H & D Folsom*)

New Worcester   (See *Torkelson Arms Co.*)

New York Arms Co.   (See *H & D Folsom*)

New York Machine Made   Hammer, laminated steel barrels. No proof marks. Sold for $60 in 1890. Nothing further known.

NEW YORK MANUFACTURERS CO.
New York, N.Y.

Sold by direct mail in 1883 breech-loading hammer gun with case, brass shells, and cleaning rod for $25.

Nichols (John)   (See *D. M. Lefever Sons & Co.*)

Nichols & Lefever   Six grades of double-barrels selling from $125 to $250. See D. M. Lefever Sons & Co.

Nitro Bird   (See *H & D Folsom*)

Nitro Hunter   Single-barrel. (See *H & D Folsom*)

Nitro Special   Single-barrel, made by Stevens Arms Co., selling at $8 in 1907.

S. S. Northcote   English made. Importer unknown.

Norwich Arms Co.   Norwich, Conn. Sears Roebuck brand sold by them in 1906, in grades of $11.72 and $13.22. Both hammer guns. See *H & D Folsom.*

Not-Nac Mfg. Co. (See *H & D Folsom*)

Occidental Belgian hammer gun. Also marked on action "The Interchangeable." Nothing further known.

Old Hickory Single barrel. Brand name Hibbard, Spencer, Bartlett Co.

Olympic Brand name Morley & Murphy Hdw. Co., Green Bay, Wisc.

OSTRANDER REPEATING GUN CO.
San Francisco, Cal.
1890–93. Pump gun. A patent of Willis H. Ostrander. Nothing further known.

Oxford Arms Co. (See *H & D Folsom*)

P & G and *Pagoma* Brand name Paxton & Gallagher Hdw. Co.

Paragon (See *H & D Folsom*)

PARK & McLEISH
Columbus, Ohio
1878–80. Made double-barrels. Reorganized as Park & Grabber. 1886–88. Nothing further known.

PARKER BROS.
Meriden, Conn.
Parker first produced shotguns about 1865, a hammer gun in 14-gauge with under-lever release. In 1882 a top-lever appeared, and the first hammerless gun was marketed in 1889. A great many different models of Parker Bros. shotguns were made and the company's history has been thoroughly researched. Those interested should refer to *Parker, America's Finest Shotgun,* by Peter H. Johnson, Bonanza Books, New York.

C. Parker & Co. (See *H & D Folsom*)

Parkhurst (See *H & D Folsom*)

PARRY FIREARMS CO.
Ithaca, New York
Made double-barrels in 1889. "Parry" was also a brand name of Wilkes-Barre Gun Co. and undoubtedly the two firms were interconnected at one time. Both were sold to Ithaca around 1898.

Peerless (See *H & D Folsom*)

Perfection (See *H & D Folsom*)

Philadelphia Arms Co. Philadelphia, Pa. (See *Ansley H. Fox*)

Phoenix   Single barrel made by Whitney Arms, New Haven, Conn., selling for $15 in 1878.

PHOENIX CO.
New York, N.Y.
Made double barrels from about 1870. In 1874 produced a 12-gauge marked "Cal. 12" with patent date "26-74."

Piedmont   (See *H & D Folsom*)

Pieper (Henri)   1880–98, Liège, Belgium. Sold many guns in several models to the U. S., the most notable being a hammer gun called "Modified Diana" for $15 in 1898. Principal importer of these guns was Cornwall & Jespersen, of New York.

Pioneer Arms Co.   (See *H & D Folsom*)

PITTSBURGH FIREARMS CO.
68 5th Avenue
Pittsburgh, Pa.
Most references say 1860–70 but known to have imported an English 10-gauge hammer gun marked "Anson & Deeley" on the rib as late as 1878.

Pittsfield   (See *H & D Folsom*)

Poultney & Sneider   (See *Poultney & Trimble Co.*)

POULTNEY & TRIMBLE CO.
200 W. Baltimore Street
Baltimore, Md.
1860–75. One of our earliest breech-loading double-barrels, built on Sneider's patent. (See *C. W. Sneider*)

Wm. Powell & Son   High grade English gun with several models used here. Maintained agency in New York during 80's and 90's.

Premier   Brand name of Montgomery Ward.

Progress   Brand name of Charles J. Godfrey Co., New York.

James Purdey & Sons   This English "Best" gun sold here in 1880's by Jos. C. Grubb & Co., 712 Market Street, Philadelphia, Pa., with their U. S. agency being Schuyler & Duane, 189 Broadway, New York.

Quail   (See *H & D Folsom*)

Queen City   (See *Elmira Arms Co.*)

Ranger   Sears Roebuck brand name. Used on several model guns by Stevens and Meriden.

Wm. Read & Sons   About 1910. Sold for $65. Nothing further known.

Red Chieftain   (See *H & D Folsom*)

Reliance   Brand name of the John Meunier Gun Co., Milwaukee, Wisc.

REMINGTON ARMS CO.
Ilion, N.Y.

Remington first made a breech-loading double-barrel in 1873. It was an Andrew Whitmore design of hammer-lifter action, and offered in three grades from $45 to $75. Both 10 and 12-gauge were made. In 1878 the design was modified and continued until the new Model 1882. There were four grades from $50 to $90. Hammerless models were offered in 1894 in various grades up to $750 for the Remington "Special." The EE grade, selling for $247.50, was certainly as fine a gun as made in America at that time.

Rev-O-Noc   (See *H & D Folsom*)

H. T. Rice   Hammerless, medium grade gun sold in 1887 by Schoverling, Daly & Gales.

Henry Richards   Both single and double-barrel. This was a second-line gun made by W. & C. Scott & Sons to be imported exclusively by J. P. Moores & Son, 302 Broadway, New York City. The double-barrel 10-gauge sold for $75 in 1881, and the single barrel 12-gauge with barrel length up to thirty-six inches, for $15.

M. Richards   Belgian made, steel barrel, hammer gun. Importer unknown.

W. Richards   (See *H & D Folsom*)

Westley Richards   Agents in the U. S. were J. Palmer O'Neil Co., Pittsburgh, Pa., who sold this famous Birmingham-made English "best" gun at prices from $190 to $450.

Richter (Charles)   (See *H & D Folsom*)

Rickard Arms Co.   (See *H & D Folsom*)

Rival   Brand name of Van Camp Hdw. Co. In 1887 was a seven and a half pound 12-gauge selling for $50 and made by N. R. Davis.

Riverside Arms Co.   Single-barrel, double-barrel, and pump guns. Made by Stevens and thought not to be used until about 1915, but perhaps earlier.

W. Roberts   Hammer gun, twist steel, engraved. Nothing further known.

Roper   Revolving shotgun, 1866 patent of Sylvester Roper, of Amherst, Mass.

Royal Gun Co.   (See *Hollenbeck Gun Co.*)

Royal Gun Works   Belgian made, hammer, laminated steel. Nothing further known.

Royal Service   (See *H & D Folsom*)

Rummel   (See *H & D Folsom*)

Ruso   (See *H & D Folsom*)

Russell Arms Co.   (See *H & D Folsom*)

S. H. Co.   Brand of Shapleigh Hdw. Co.

St. Louis Arms Co.   (See *H & D Folsom*)

SCHAEFER, WM. R., & SONS
61 Elm Street
Boston, Mass.

1872–79. "Makers fine hammer and hammerless double-barrels to order only." Other advertising of this firm declared "Manufacturer only of first-class breech-loading shotguns." Known to have made the "Wm. R. Schaefer" hammer gun under patents of Schaefer and Julius Elston. This firm also did extensive gunsmithing, rebarreling, and conversions from percussion to breach-loading.

V. Chr. Schilling   This gun made in Suhl, Prussia, most commonly in 16-gauge, which sold with fine damascus barrels and case for $125 in 1881.

SCHNADER, FRANK K.
Redding, Pa.

Uncertain, but not believed to have made entire gun. They were barrel makers for Great Western Gun Works, of Pittsburgh, around 1884, and branded barrels with their name.

SCHUYLER, HARTLEY & GRAHAM
19 Maiden Lane, 20 & 22 John Street
New York, N.Y.

1861–76. This firm was known as America's greatest sporting goods dealer. Not believed to have actually manufactured shotguns, but did sell imported guns under their brand. They were also agents for W. & C. Scott & Sons, J. P. Clabrough & Bro., P. Webley & Sons, and Westley Richards, among others. (Also see *Hartley & Graham*)

I. A. Scott   Hammer, 10-gauge, thirty-three and a half inch Damascus, engraved pheasants on each side of action. Nothing further known.

W. & C. Scott & Sons Most widely known and used of "Best" grade English shotguns in America during the "Golden Age." A favorite of champion live-bird shooters of that day. Made in many grades. Henry C. Squires was principal agent in America during this period.

Wm. P. Scott English made hammer, Damascus. Sold by J. W. Hutchison, 81 Chambers Street, New York. Scott's "American Field" model sold in 1883 for $50 in 12-gauge and $5 more for 10-gauge.

SEARS, HENRY, & CO.
88 Lake Street
Chicago, Ill.

Distributors and gunsmiths. Sold hammer guns branded with their name during mid-80's.

SHATTUCK, C. S., ARMS CO.
Hatfield, Mass.

1878–1908. This firm known mostly for single-barrel guns in gauges 8, 10, 12, and 16. They were made hammer, hammerless, and "trigger action." Earliest model called "American" and models in the 90's sold under the name "Champion." Most guns in the $7 to $15 price range. In 1899 offered a hammerless double-barrel with twist barrels at $25. Firm was formerly Hyde & Shattuck.

The Sheffield Belgian made for Baldwin & Co., Ltd., New Orleans, La.

Shelton's Challenge Gun Made in New Haven, Conn. 1883 from patents of Clark R. Shelton. Hammer double-barrel with auxiliary barrel inserts for different chokes and rifle calibers.

Shue's Special (See *H & D Folsom*)

Sickel's Arms Co. (See *H & D Folsom*)

Simplex (See *Tobin Arms Co.*)

Simpson Iver Johnson-made single barrel. Do not confuse with German "Simpson."

Smith (Dexter) Springfield, Mass. Made limited quantity double-barrels in 1874.

SMITH, L. C., GUN CO.
Syracuse, N.Y.

The "L. C. Smith" was one of the most highly regarded American made double-barrels of its era. The first Smith, of Baker design, appeared in 1878. It was redesigned by Alexander Brown about 1883. A hammerless model was offered beginning about 1888. The "Smith" was a side-lock gun famous for its rotary bolt. This gun has been made in many grades, as well as special models. A Baker designed three-barrel gun was also made, and discontinued in 1880. Lyman Smith sold his interests to the Hunter Arms Co., of Fulton, N.Y., in 1890 who continued to make the L. C. Smith line of shotguns. The Hunter Arms Co. was eventually purchased by Marlin, who in 1969 again started production of the "L. C. Smith."

SMITH, OTIS A.
Rockfall, Conn.

Double-barrels so marked. Nothing further known about shotgun production of this firm famous for their revolvers.

SMITH & WESSON
Springfield, Mass.

The famous revolver makers produced a seven and a half pound 12 Ga. hammer double-barrel under their 1867 patents. Quantity made unknown, but must have been very few. Marked S & W from #215, before that "Wesson."

SNEIDER, CHARLES W.
214 W. Pratt Street
Baltimore, Md.

Made double barrels under joint patents of Charles W. and Charles Edward Sneider from 1875 to 1887. Guns selling in a price range of $50 to $300, and in gauges 4, 8, 10, 12, 14, 16, and 20. Both hammer and hammerless models were offered during this period with one model brand-named "American Hammerless," a sidelock gun with adjustable main spring. The firm's name was changed in 1882 to Clark & Sneider. They also altered muzzle guns to breechloaders for which the "Sneider System" became the most famous of five American systems.

Southern Arms Co.   (See *H & D Folsom*)
Special Service   (See *H & D Folsom*)
SPENCER ARMS CO.

This firm produced the Roper shotgun in Hartford, Conn., in 1868, and also the first successful American pump gun, "The Spencer." Later reorganized as Billings & Spencer Co. The Spencer pump gun was made in both a solid frame and take-down model. Made in Windsor, Conn., 1882-89. They sold in grades from less than $40 to Grade A at $100. While most production was 12-gauge, a few were made in 10-gauge. Spencer patents were then bought by Francis Bannerman and the "Bannerman" model made in Brooklyn, N.Y. from 1890 to 1907. Bannerman offered the Spencer machinery to Union Arms Co., of Toledo, Ohio, in 1902 and they advertised as makers of the

Spencer pump gun. However, this was premature as the deal fell through with Bannerman and no guns are known to have actually been produced by Union Arms.

Spencer Gun Co.   Double barrel. (See *H & D Folsom*)

Sportsman   (See *H & D Folsom*)

Springfield Arms Co.   (See *H & D Folsom*)

Square Deal   (See *H & D Folsom*)

SQUIRES, HENRY C.
1 Cortland Street
New York, N.Y.
Was long-time U. S. agent for Greener guns. Also sold guns under their own brand name.

STAFFORD, J. F.
Wichita, Kans.
Either made or branded hammerless guns in 1887.

Standard Arms Co.   Brand name of Fisher's, of New York City, for English and Belgian hammer guns selling in 1878 from $32 to $48.

Stanley   (See *H & D Folsom*)

Star Leader   Hammer double-barrel. Nothing further known.

State Arms Co.   (See *H & D Folsom*)

H. J. Sterling   (See *H & D Folsom*)

STEVENS, J., ARMS & TOOL CO.
Chickopee Falls, Mass.
Made their first double-barrel in 1876, a hammer gun with two "trigger guards," the front one acting as breech opener. At various times made double hammer guns selling at $15, hammerless at $20, single-barrels at $8, all these in the 1890's. Made various other models double and single-barrel, as well as pump guns, shortly after 1900. The firm was partially acquired in 1920 by Savage Arms, and completely so by 1936. The Stevens name continues today on guns made by Savage.

STRONG FIREARMS CO.
New Haven, Conn.
Made the Dickerman single-barrel about 1880. Firm acquired by Winchester in 1881. (See *Amos Dickerman*)

Sullivan Arms Co.   (See *H & D Folsom*)

SUTHERLAND'S, S., & SONS
Richmond, Va.

1856–76. Known for fine grade muzzle-loading guns but said to have also produced a breechloader under their name, although it is possible these guns were only conversions.

Syco   (See *H & D Folsom*)

SYRACUSE ARMS CO.
Syracuse, N.Y.

Firm produced under the above name from about 1888–1908. Was eventually absorbed by Ithaca Gun Co. Prior to 1888 was known as the Syracuse Forging & Gun Co. Syracuse Arms Co. made hammerless guns under patents of Frank Hollenbeck and G. A. Horne. Also made guns for Sears Roebuck under Sears and other brand names. The "Hollenbeck" model sold in 1897 for $27 in the hammer model; and $33, hammerless. The "Syracuse" model was made in 10, 12, 16, and 20 gauges. There were eight grades, the 00 grade at $30, to Grade D at $475. All guns from $75 up had Whitworth fluid steel barrels and auto ejectors. Syracuse is believed to be the original financial backer of the Hollenbeck three-barrel gun. (See *Hollenbeck Gun Co.*)

Ten Star and *Ten Star Heavy Duty*   (See *H & D Folsom*)

Texas Ranger   Montgomery Ward brand name.

Thames Arms Co.   Shotgun brand name of Harrington & Richardson. No known connection with Thames Arms Co., of Norwich, Conn.

Three-Barrel Gun Co.   (See *Hollenbeck Gun Co.*)

Tiger   (See *H & D Folsom*)

Tiping & Lawden   English-made 10-gauge, 32″ damascus, eleven and a half pounds, selling for $200 in 1881. Also 12 gauge guns of good quality.

TOBIN ARMS CO.
Norwich, Conn. and Woodstock, Ontario

Hammerless, steel barreled double-barrels in 12 and 16-gauge, first appearing about 1905. The company seems to have been in business only some three or four years, but guns were assembled from parts much later by G. B. Crandall. Also made model called "Tobin Simplex."

Tolley   Birmingham made by J & W Tolley's and first sold in America by a branch office of the firm at 29 Maiden Lane, New York City. Prices in 1874 were: Pioneer grade, $65; Tolley, $90; Standard, $115; National,

$140; Challenge, $180; and Paragon, $225. By 1887 a hammerless model was sold by Schoverling, Daly & Gales.

TONKS, JOSEPH
Boston, Mass.

About 1860 to 1882. First known for high quality muzzle-loading guns and later breechloaders. According to Fred Kimble, Mr. Tonks bored the first commercial shotgun choke in America. He was later connected with Whitmore Gun Co., of Malden, Mass.

TORKELSON ARMS CO.
Worcester, Mass.

Made "New Worcester" hammerless with double-twist steel barrels.

Trap   English made by Enos James. Sold by Henry C. Squires.

Traps Best   (See *H & D Folsom*)

Triumph   Sears Roebuck brand name. (See *H & D Folsom*)

U. S. Arms Co.   (See *H & D Folsom*)

U. S. ARMS & CUTLERY CO.
Rochester, N.Y.

Known for knives and pistols, but produced a few double-barrels.

UNION ARMS CO.
Toledo, Ohio

In business about 1902–04. Company was formed to produce the "Spencer Pump Gun" using machinery of the old Spencer Arms Co. which was to be purchased from Francis Bannerman. The sale was never consumated and the firm did not actually produce Spencer guns. They did, however, have a pump gun made for them bearing their name, with actions thought to have been made by Bostwick-Braun Co., of Toledo. The barrels were made by the German Essen Works, of Krupp. It is also reported some pump gun actions were made for them by Marlin. They furnished Sears Roebuck with imported guns bearing the Union Arms Co. name and which were sold by Sears for $18.75.

Utica Firearms Co.   Hammer double-barrel. Nothing further known.

Victor and *Victor Special*   (See *H & D Folsom*)

The Victoria   Hammer, twist barrels. Sold for $35 in 1883 by Henry C. Squires.

Virginia Arms Co.   (See *H & D Folsom*)

Volunteer   (See *H & D Folsom*)

Vulcan Arms Co. (See *H & D Folsom*)

R. Wakefield English made, but designed and sold by R. H. Kilby, Montreal, Canada, in 1877.

Warren Arms Co. (See *H & D Folsom*)

Wautauga (See *H & D Folsom*)

Webley English made, high quality. Schuyler, Hartley & Graham were American agents. Gun was later "Webley & Scott."

WESSON FIREARMS CO.
Springfield, Mass.
1864–68. Later Frank Wesson, Worcester, Mass. Single barrels of good quality.

WESTERN ARMS & CARTRIDGE CO.
108 Madison Street
Chicago, Ill.
Formerly the A. G. Spalding Co. They used brand "Western A. & C. Co." on imported guns around 1887.

Western Long Range Montgomery Ward brand name.

Wheeling 3-Barrel Gun Co. (See *Hollenbeck Arms Co.*)

Whippet (See *H & D Folsom*)

White Powder Wonder Sears Roebuck brand name for single barrel, selling for $7 in 1898.

Whitmore (See *American Arms Co.*)

WHITNEY ARMS CO.
New Haven, Conn.
To 1888. One of first American firms to produce double-barreled guns in quantity. Also made the "Howard" and "Phoenix" single-barrel guns, both rifled and smooth bore. (Also see *H & D Folsom*)

WHITNEY SAFETY FIREARMS CO.
Florence, Mass.
1891–94. Made double-barrels, sold through Charles J. Godfrey.

WILKES-BARRE GUN CO.
Wilkes-Barre, Pa.
Made hammer and hammerless with top grade selling for $125 in 1892. Also made guns for the trade under many brand names.

Wilkinson Arms Co. (See *H & D Folsom*)

Fred K. Williams English made and imported by several different firms.

Williams & Powell A "Best" grade English gun with their 1885 Model "Triplex Grip" hammerless widely used by live-bird shooters.

Wilmont Arms Co. (See *H & D Folsom*)

Wilshire Arms Co. (See *H & D Folsom*)

Wiltshire Arms Co. (See *H & D Folsom*)

WINCHESTER REPEATING ARMS CO.
New Haven, Conn.

From 1879 to 1884 Winchester sold six grades of hammer guns from $40 to $85 in price. They were all English made by various firms — W. C. McEntree & Co., Richard Rodman, Bonehill, and W. C. Scott & Sons — but all bore the brand "Winchester Repeating Arms Co." About 10,000 were imported and sold only through Winchester's New York store. Sale by Winchester was discontinued about 1884 and the guns left in stock were sold to John P. Moore's Sons, which was later Schoverling, Daly & Gales. Before 1900, Winchester made the Model 1893 and 1897 pump guns, as well as the 1887 lever action.

Winfield Arms Co. (See *H & D Folsom*)

Winoca Arms Co. (See *H & D Folsom*)

Wolverine Arms Co. (See *H & D Folsom*)

Worthington Arms Co. (See *H & D Folsom*)

WRIGHT ARMS CO.
Lawrence, Mass.

Known for muzzleloading 8 gauges, but imported Belgian breechloading double-barrels bearing their name in 1878.

XL Hopkins & Allen brand name.

YOUNG REPEATING ARMS CO.
Columbus, Ohio

1894–1906. A pump-action gun designed by "Sparrow" Young, a well-known trapshooter of that time.

Zulu This name applied to many early single-barrels of uncertain origin and selling in the $5 to $10 price range. But most often used to refer to the Sneider rifle action when converted to shotguns. Many cheap copies were made abroad.

[APPENDIX B]

Bibliography

MUCH of the information in this book was obtained from private records and collections of gun clubs, manufacturers, and individuals, but many rare and out-of-print publications were also consulted. These can be found on the shelves of larger libraries, and also appear occasionally in the lists of sporting-book dealers. For those with a further interest in the "Golden Age" I particularly recommend the following:

Askins, Chas., *The American Shotgun*. New York, Outing Publishing Co., 1910.
————, *Wing Shooting*. Chicago, Outers' Book Co., 1923.
Barber, Joel, *Wildfowl Decoys*. New York, Windward House, 1934.
"Blue Rock" (Captain A. W. Money), *Pigeon Shooting*. New York, Shooting & Fishing, 1896.
Bogardus, A. H., *Field, Cover & Trapshooting*. New York, J. B. Ford, 1874.
Bumstead, John, *On the Wing*. New York, Happy Hours, 1869.
"Chipmunk," *Wing Shooting*. London, Ont., T. G. Davey, 1881.
Connett, E. V., *Duck Shooting Along the Atlantic Tidewater*. New York, Wm. Morrow & Co., 1947.
Eaton, D. H., *Trapshooting*. Cincinnati, Sportsmens Review Pub. Co., 1918.

"Gloan" (T. A. Logan), *Breech-Loaders.* New York, Orange Judd Co., 1873.

Greener, W. W., *Choke-Bore Guns and How to Load For All Kinds of Game.* London and New York, Cassell, Petter & Galpin, 1876.

————, *The Gun and Its Development* (Ninth ed., 1969 reprint). New York, Bonanza, 1881.

Grinnell, G. B., *American Duck Shooting.* New York, Forest & Stream Pub. Co., 1901.

————, *American Game Bird Shooting.* New York, Forest & Stream Pub. Co., 1910.

Guinotte, J. E., *Twenty Years of Trapshooting in Missouri.* Kansas City, Lawton & Burnap, 1898.

Hallock, Chas., *Sportsman's Gazetteer & General Guide.* New York, Forest & Stream Pub. Co., 1877.

Hazelton, W. C., *Supreme Duck Shooting Stories.* Chicago, Hazelton, 1936.

————, *Tales of Duck and Goose Shooting.* Springfield, Hazelton, 1922.

Lancaster, Chas., *The Art of Shooting.* London, 1890.

Leffingwell, W. B., *The Art of Wing Shooting.* Chicago, Rand McNally, 1894.

————, *Shooting on Upland, Marsh & Stream.* New York, Rand McNally, 1890.

————, *Wildfowl Shooting.* New York, Rand McNally, 1890.

Long, J. W., *American Wild-Fowl Shooting.* New York, J. B. Ford, 1874.

Murphy, J. M., *American Game Bird Shooting.* New York, Orange Judd Co., 1882.

Parmalee, Paul W., and Loomis, Forrest D., *Decoys and Decoy Carvers of Illinois.* DeKalb, Northern Illinois University Press, 1969.

Price, Gwynne, *The Gun, and How to Use It.* St. Louis News, 1884.

Pringle, J. J., *Twenty Years Snipe Shooting.* New York, Knickerbocker, 1899.

Schley, Frank, *American Partridge & Pheasant Shooting.* Frederick, Md., Baughman Brothers, 1877.

Teasdale-Buckell, G. T., *Experts on Guns and Shooting.* London, Sampson Low, Marston, & Co., 1900.

PERIODICALS

Sporting papers and magazines of the 1870-1900 era:
American Field
Arms and the Man
The (London) Field
Forest & Stream
Recreation Magazine
Spirit of the Times
Turf, Field & Farm

Trap Shooting Rules of the Golden Age

HURLINGHAM CLUB SHOOTING RULES
(REVISED TO 1895)

(The rules of the Hurlingham Club of England governed live bird shooting in America for most of its active span before and after 1900.)

1. The referee's decision shall be final.

2. (It was formerly that a shooter should hold the butt of his gun below the armpit until he called "Pull." That rule has been abolished.)

3. A missfire is not shot, under any circumstances.

4. If the shooter's gun missfire with the first barrel and he use the second and miss, the bird is to be scored lost.

5. If the missfire occurs with the second barrel, the shooter having failed to kill with his first, he may claim another bird; but he must fire off the first barrel with the cap on, and a full charge of powder, before firing the second.

6. The shooter's feet shall be behind the shooting mark until after his gun is discharged. If, in the opinion of the referee, the shooter is balked

by any antagonist or looker-on, or by the trapper, whether by accident or otherwise, he may be allowed another bird.

7. The shooter, when at his mark ready to shoot, shall give the caution, "Are you ready?" to the puller, and then call "Pull." Should the trap be pulled without the word being given, the shooter may take the bird or not; but if he fires, the bird must be deemed to be taken.

8. If, on the trap being pulled, the bird does not rise, it is at the option of the shooter to take it or not; if not, he must declare it by saying, "No bird;" but should he fire after declaring, it is not to be scored for or against him.

9. Each bird must be recovered within the boundary, if required by any party interested, or it must be scored lost.

10. If a bird that has been shot at perches or settles on the top of the fence, or on any part of the building than the fence, it is to be scored a lost bird.

11. If a bird once out of the ground should return and fall dead within the boundary, it must be scored a lost bird.

12. If the shooter advances to the mark and orders the trap to be pulled, and does not shoot at the bird, or his gun is not properly loaded, or does not go off, owing to his own negligence, that bird is to be scored lost.

13. A bird shot on the ground with the first barrel is "no bird," but it may be shot on the ground with the second barrel, if it has been fired at with the first barrel while on the wing; but if the shooter misses with the first and discharges his second barrel, it is to be accounted a lost bird, in case of not falling within bounds.

14. All birds must be gathered by the dog or trapper, and no member shall have the right ot gather his own bird, or to touch it with his hand or gun.

15. In single shooting, if more than one bird is liberated, the shooter may call "no bird," and claim another shot; but if he shoots, he must abide by the consequences.

16. The shooter must not leave the shooting mark under any pretense to follow any bird that will not rise, nor may he return to his mark, after having once quitted it, to fire his second barrel.

17. Any shooter found to have in his gun more shot than is allowed, is to be at once disqualified. Any loader supplying in sweepstakes or matches, cartridges loaded in excess of the authorized charge, will be dismissed from the club grounds.

18. None but members can shoot except on the occasion of private matches.

19. No wire cartridges or concentrators allowed, or other substance to be mixed with the shot.

20. In all handicaps, sweepstakes or matches, the standard bore of the gun is No. 12. Members shooting with less, to go at the rate of a half a yard for every bore less than 12 down to 16-bore; 11-bore gun to stand back half a yard from the handicap distance, and no guns over 11-bore allowed.

21. The winner of sweepstake of the value of ten sovereigns, including his own stake, goes back two yards; under that sum one yard, provided there be five shooters. Members saving or dividing in an advertised event will be handicapped accordingly.

22. Should any member kill a bird at a distance nearer than that at which he is handicapped, it shall be scored no bird; but should he miss, a lost bird.

23. One and a quarter ounces of shot, and four drams of black powder, or its equivalent in any other description of gunpowder, is the maximum charge. Sizes of shot restricted to Nos. 5, 6, 7 and 8.

24. All muzzle-loaders shall be loaded with shot from the club bowls.

25. If any bird escapes through any opening in the paling, it shall be "no bird."

26. From the first of May the advertised events shall begin at three o'clock, unless otherwise notified, and no shooter will be admitted after the second round in any advertised event.

27. No scouting allowed on the club premises, and no pigeons to be shot at in the shooting ground, except by the shooter standing at his mark. Anyone infringing this rule will be fined one pound.

28. Members can plate guns up till three o'clock, but not whilst sweepstakes or matches are being shot.

Rules for Double Rise

1. In double shooting, when more than two traps are pulled, the shooter may call "No birds" and claim two more, but if he shoots, he must abide by the consequences.

2. If on the traps being pulled, the birds do not rise, it is at the option of the shooter to take them or not. If not, he must declare by saying "No birds."

3. If, on the traps being pulled, one bird does not rise, he cannot demand another double rise; but he must wait and take the bird when it flies.

4.   A bird shot on the ground, if the other bird is missed, is a lost bird; but if the other bird is killed, the shooter may demand another two birds.

5.   If the shooter's gun misses fire with the first barrel, he may demand another two birds; but if he fires his second barrel, he must abide by the consequences. If the missfire occurs with the second barrel, the shooter having killed with the first, he may demand another bird, but may only use one barrel; if he missed with his first barrel, Rule five, in single shooting, will apply.

NEW YORK SPORTSMEN'S CLUB RULES

(The first widely recognized rules of live bird shooting originated in America were those of the New York Sportsmen's Club, said to have first been set about 1866.)

JUDGES

1st.   All matches or sweepstakes to be under the direction of two judges, to be appointed by the parties interested from members of the Club; and in the event of any difference of opinion between them, they are to choose a referee, whose decision shall be final.

TRAPS

2d.   Ground-traps are to be used, unless otherwise agreed upon by the parties interested.

3d.   In shooting with two traps, the choice of either must be decided by lot.

4th.   In double-bird shooting, two traps must be used, unless otherwise agreed upon, placed six feet apart, and the lines so attached that both traps may be pulled together.

GUNS

5th.   The use of single or double barrelled guns to be specified at the time of making a match, or entering a sweepstakes.

SHOT

6th.   The *weight of shot* not to exceed one and a half ounces either for single or double birds.

7TH.   Any person or persons using a greater weight of shot than this, unless an increase of it shall have been specified or agreed upon, loses his claim in the result of the match, or sweepstakes, as the case may be.

RISE

8TH.   The *rise* for single birds to be twenty-one yards, and for double birds eighteen yards.

BOUNDARIES

9TH.   The *boundary* for single birds to be eighty yards and for double birds one hundred yards; the distances being measured from the trap.

10TH.   If a bird is once out of bounds, it is missed.

SCORING

11TH.   When a person is at the *score,* and ready to shoot, he is to call *pull;* and should the trap be sprung without his having given the word, he may take the bird or birds or not; but if he shoots, the bird or birds will be charged to him.

12TH.   The party at the score must not leave it to shoot.

13TH.   The party shooting is to be at the score within the expiration of five minutes from the last shot; but in the event of any delay beyond his control, he may claim fifteen minutes once in the course of a match or sweepstakes.

14TH.   When a party is at the score, no one will be permitted to go in front of him to put a bird up, in the event of its not rising readily.

15TH.   The party at the score must hold the but of his gun below his elbow, until the bird or birds rise.

RISING OF BIRDS

16TH.   If the trap or traps are sprung, and the bird or birds do not rise in a reasonable time, either of the judges may declare "no bird"; but if they do not say "no bird," the party at the score must wait for the bird or birds to rise.

17TH.   In double-bird shooting, should only one bird fly, it is to be charged to the party shooting, whether he may have shot or not.

18TH.   Should two birds be killed with one barrel, they are to be credited to the party shooting.

19TH.   If a bird or birds walk away from the trap, the judges may declare "no bird."

20TH.   A bird must be on the wing when shot at.

MISSING FIRE

21ST.   In case a percussion-cap or primer, as the case may be, fails to explode, the bird or birds are not to be charged to the party shooting; but if the cap or primer explodes without igniting a charge, or if, after his giving the word to pull, his gun proves not to have been cocked, or not to have been properly loaded, and it fails to fire, he will be held to have missed.

BALKING

22D.   If, in the opinion of the judges, the party at the score is balked, or in any manner obstructed by his opponent, or any person other than his own backers, he may be allowed to trap another bird, in accordance with the decision of the judges.

23RD.   In single-bird shooting, when more than one rises at a time, either of the judges may call "no bird," if he or they think proper; but if the party at the score has shot at a bird, it will be charged to him.

24TH.   If a bird or birds shall fly towards the parties within the bounds, in such a manner that to shoot at them would involve the wounding of any of the parties referred to, the judges, or either of them, may decide "no bird."

25TH.   If a bird in its flight is shot at by another party than the one at the score, and is recovered within the bounds, the judges are to decide if the bird was missed by the party at the score.

26TH.   If at any time it should so occur that different and opposing orders should be given by the judges to a party at the score, he is to arrest his fire; and any bird shot at by him after such orders shall not be allowed him if recovered, or charged to him if missed.

TIES

27TH.   In case of a *tie,* it must be shot off the same day, if practicable to do so, unless the purse, or prizes, are divided by agreement; and if not, it must be decided the *first* ensuing fitting day.

28TH.   In the decision of ties, three shots will be required both for double and single birds, except otherwise agreed upon.

[172]

Appendix C

RECOVERING OF BIRDS

29TH.   The party shooting must gather his birds individually, if required to do so by his opponent.

30TH.   The party recovering a bird must use his hands alone.

31ST.   If a bird alights in a tree, or upon any place impracticable to be conveniently recovered, the party shooting will be allowed fifteen minutes for the bird to fall or change his resting-place; if he is not recovered in that time, it will be held to be a missed bird.

THE FLYING CLAY PIGEON
RULES FOR SHOOTING

The following are the first set of rules for clay pigeon shooting. They were devised by the Ligowsky Company and accompanied each Ligowsky trap sold from 1880 to about four years later.

RULE I: *Traps and Rise* — All matches shall be shot from screened traps. Rise for single and double birds to be ten yards. In double bird shooting the traps shall be placed four to six feet apart. The direction of the flight of bird shall be varied for each consecutive shot.

RULE II: *Scoring* — When a person is at the score and ready to shoot, he shall call "Pull," and should the trap be sprung without his having given the word, or, in single bird shooting should more than one bird raise at a time, he may take the bird, *or* birds, or not; but if he shoots, the bird or birds shall be charged to him. The party at the score must not leave it to shoot, and must hold the butt of his gun below his elbow until the bird or birds rise; and in case of infraction of this provision, the bird or birds shall be scored as missed.

RULE III: *Rising of Birds* — The shooter, when he is at his mark ready to shoot, shall give the caution, "Are you ready?" to the puller, and then say "Pull." Should the trap be pulled without the word being given the shooter may take the bird or not; but if he fires, the bird shall be said to be taken. If, on the trap being pulled, the bird does not rise three feet high and ten yards distance, it is at the option of the shooter to take it or not; if not, he must declare it by saying "No bird"; but should he fire after declaring, it is not to be scored for or against him.

[173]

Rule IV: All birds must be broken in the air to count; that is, the shot must knock at least a plainly perceptible piece out of the bird in the air, otherwise it shall be called a lost bird.

Rule V: There shall be no restriction as to size of shot used (7 and 8 are recommended), or charge of powder (three and a quarter to four and a half drams recommended), but the charge of shot shall not exceed one an a quarter oz. Dixon measure. Anyone using larger quantity of shot shall forfeit all rights in the matches. After a gun is loaded and challenged, and the shooter discharges his gun, the penalty will be the same as for overloading.

Rule VI: *Flight of Birds* — In single shooting, if more than one bird is liberated, the shooter may call "No bird," and claim another shot; but if he shoots he must abide by the consequences. In double shooting both birds shall be on the wing when the first is shot at. If but one bird flies, and but one barrel is fired or snapped, the birds shall in no wise be scored, whether hit or missed, but the party shooting shall have two more birds; or if both birds fly and are broken with one barrel, he must shoot at two other birds.

Rule VII: *Ties* — In case of a tie at single birds, the distance shall be increased five yards, and shall be shot off at the five birds. In case of a second tie, the distance shall again be increased five yards, and this distance shall be maintained till the match is decided. The ties in double bird shooting shall be shot off at five double rises. Ties shot off at fifteen yards rise, at three pair birds each, and in case of second ties, three more pairs each at twenty yards rise, and so on until decided. In all cases both traps must be sprung at the same time.

Rule VIII: *Time at the Score* — A participant in a match shall hold himself in readiness to come to the score when his name is called by the scorer. If he is longer than five minutes, it shall be discretionary with the referee whether he shall allow him to proceed further in the match or not.

Rule IX: *Miss-fire* — Should gun miss-fire or fail to discharge, from any cause, it shall score as a lost bird, unless the referee finds, upon examination, that the gun was properly loaded, and the miss-fire unavoidable, in which case he shall allow another bird.

Rule X: *Loading Guns* — In case of breech-loaders, the party called to the score shall not place his cartridge in the gun until he arrives at the score. In case of muzzle-loaders, the party called to the score shall not place the cap on his gun until he arrives at the score. No one but a contestant has a right to challenge.

RULE XI: *Judges and Referee* — Two judges and a referee shall be appointed before the shooting commences. The referee's decision shall be final. He shall have power to call "No bird" in case any bird fails to fly, and may allow a contestant another bird in case the latter shall have been interfered with, or may, for any reason satisfactory to the referee, be entitled to it. If a bird shall fly toward parties within the bounds in such a manner that to shoot at it would endanger any person, another bird may be allowed; and if a bird is shot at by any person besides the party at the score, the referee shall decide how it shall be scored, whether a new bird shall be allowed.